ESSEX
in 1950

DESERT ISLAND BOOKS   *www.desertislandbooks.com*

ESSEX
in 1950

by
C HENRY WARREN

SERIES EDITOR: CLIVE LEATHERDALE

Desert Island Books Limited

First Published in 1950
as "Essex"
by Robert Hale

This edition published in 2000
by
DESERT ISLAND BOOKS LIMITED
89 Park Street, Westcliff-on-Sea, Essex SS0 7PD
United Kingdom
www.desertislandbooks.com

British Library Cataloguing-in-Publication Data
A catalogue record for this book is available from
the British Library

ISBN 1-874287-42-2

Printed in Great Britain
by
Redwood Books, Trowbridge, Wiltshire

Contents

Editor's Note

For those interested in the history of the county of Essex, few books come as highly recommended as Clarence Henry Warren's *Essex*. Published in 1950, to the modern eye, the world that Warren describes appears irretrievably remote. Yet this comes as no surprise. After all, over the past fifty years the world has changed at a pace never before witnessed. The readers of today can therefore be forgiven, as they browse through these pages, for wondering whether the Essex of 1950 bears any meaningful resemblance to the county as it is today.

The Essex before Warren's eyes is one that has slipped from our grasp and even from our memory. Only readers of middle age and over can have any direct recall of the customs and superstitions that Warren so vividly describes. For younger readers, this Essex in which "rurality is all" has no connection with the rampant urbanisation of the Essex in which they now live. Nowhere is this highlighted so strikingly than in Warren's simple observation that, "if you cannot take an intelligent interest in stock and crops, you are a lost man in Essex; and if you cannot talk of these willingly and almost exclusively, all day and every day, you will soon be talking to yourself."

What makes this book so valuable is Warren's ability to let us reach out and touch this lost Essex. We can view the county as our parents and grandparents saw it, and understand the myths and superstitions that shaped their lives. Today's residents of Coggeshall will learn why to call something a "Coggeshall job" would bring derision on their forefathers, and that deep in the mists of history Kelvedon acquired a reputation for ill-repute.

Perhaps the most important insight in this book is that into the mind of its author. Warren was born in the late Victorian age, and the gentlemanly elegance which flows through these pages has similarly vanished. To read both his words and his revelations into bygone Essex are a pleasure which the modern reader should savour.

Gayle Newman
Desert Island Books

CHAPTER 1

Introductory View

"THE worse for the rider, the better for the bider" is an old
Essex saying that had its origin in the days when Essex
roads were notoriously ill-kept. It still has a certain applicabil-
ity today, though the traveller goes by train or motor-car. There
are places in Essex that take the best part of half a day to get to
by train from London, whilst the tortuous nature of the lanes
and by-ways is a sufficient deterrent to the hasty motorist.
Perhaps the rider-and-bider saying is not in actual use any
longer, but the sense of it is often intended by zealous Essex-
lovers. "Essex?" says the unadventurous stranger, and not
without scorn. "But it is so difficult to get at." And our ready
agreement implies, perhaps, that we even prefer it to be so.

For the outstanding thing about Essex, especially the northern half of it, is the way in which it remains, in spite of
progress, unspoiled. London is only just over the horizon: its
dormitories, like a spreading stain, run far into the interior. Yet
at its best Essex remains as resolutely rural as if it were the
other side of the country. Typical is the fact that its dialect
(which only the too refined ear could dislike) is almost as much
in use as it was half a century ago. Even the children, though a
'bus now takes them to school in the towns, where urbanised
teachers instruct them in the use of so-called King's English,
tend to revert to their native tongue directly they have leapt off
the 'bus and clicked the cottage gate behind them. And their
parents and grandparents, out in the fields or by their firesides,
use words which have not changed since the Essex "Hodge" was
a Saxon serf.

Tenacity is an outstanding trait of the Essex character. Some
might call it obstinacy or even churlishness. Rather, I think, it
is the innate conservatism of men and women who have always
lived on the land – and clay land at that. They move slowly, in
time as in place. They know that progress is too often only
another name for the royal road – man's persistent endeavour to

reap his rewards with a minimum of effort. And they know, out
of centuries of bitter struggle, that at any rate as far as the land
is concerned there really is no royal road. The longest way
round often proves the quickest in the end. "There never was
somethin' for nothin'," says my neighbour, true Essex toiler of
the fields; "and that ain't likely there ever will be." The curse of
Adam is in such sentiments.

And so, what with the inadequacy of its means of communication and the conservatism of its natives, Essex remains as
genuinely rural, at least in its hinterland, as the furthermost
corners of our island. Admittedly the planners, with their dream
of satellite towns and focal villages, would seem determined
that this state of affairs shall not go on; but how far will they
succeed? I used to fear that the recent war would have a radical
effect on the Essex rural character. When there were aerodromes all over the county and every village pub, even in the
remotest village, was crowded with Americans, it seemed inevitable that a close contact with this quick, nervous race of
gadget-minded men would leave its mark on the slow, tenacious,
intuitive Essex character. But the crops are growing on the
aerodromes again (or at least on some of them) and I cannot say
that I have noticed any fundamental change in the men who are
left to till them. And so perhaps, in spite of progress and the
planners, Essex will continue to be the Home County with a
difference.

That, anyway, is the impression one gets almost anywhere
north of Chelmsford. With Thaxted for centre – or Dunmow, or
Witham, or Braintree, or Maldon – one can go far in any direction without once losing the sense that here is rural England at
its best. The intensively cultivated farmlands of Essex offer as
pleasant a scenery as any in the land. Time was, I realise, when
only a Cobbett, for whom scenery was to be judged more by its
well-tilled fields than by its wild grandeur, could have got away
with such a statement; but we are all more or less able to appreciate a man-made landscape today. If we are not, then the best
of Essex is lost on us. It is no use seeking grandeur or rarity
here. Three hundred feet above sea-level is about the most
Essex can boast in the way of heights; it has no sparkling
brooks, no rainbow'd waterfalls, and even its wild flowers are
mainly confined to the commoner sort and those that are
indigenous to arable. Nevertheless, its claim to possess a pleas-

ant scenery is more than justified; but it is the scenery of man's
devising – the fair prospect offered where man has concentrated
his genius through generations on a wise co-operation with
nature for the production of crop and stock.

Did not John Norden, away back in Tudor times, say of
Essex that "this shire is moste fatt, frutefull, and full of profitable thinges, exceeding anie other shire for the general
comodeties and the plentie, (so that it) seemeth to me to deserve
the title of the english Goshen, the fattest of the Lande: compa-
rable to Palestina, that flowed with milke and hunnye"? And so,
if less flowerily, it might be said of Essex today. The county lies
largely in the corn belt and has a tradition of good husbandry
based on the old Norfolk four-course rotation of roots, barley,
clover, wheat. Nowhere would you have found before the war a
stricter concern, on everybody's part, farmer and farm-hand
alike, for the welfare of the land. Nowhere would you have
found the life of the community more closely integrated, as
formerly it was all over the country, with the activities of the
fields. In fact, when all is said, enjoyment of the Essex scene is
based upon an ability to appreciate just this: Essex *is* farming.

Rurality is all. Even the towns – Ongar, Halstead, Epping,
Thaxted – are still essentially rural, in the sense that they owe
the most and best of their existence to the surrounding villages,
as these do, in turn, to the surrounding fields. As you wander
down the streets, a bee or a butterfly may overtake you, or you
may smell above the traffic fumes the dry, floury odour of
ripening corn. Likely as not, the talk you overhear on the pave-
ments and in the shops and pubs will be of farming matters.
And even if there are fish fries and petrol pumps and picture
houses, these detract nothing – why should they? – from the
prevailing rural character. Thaxted, for instance, so it is said,
was once a prosperous centre of the steel industry, "the Sheffield of the South," in whose furnaces not coal but good Essex
oak was burned. But today Thaxted is all that Sheffield is not
and nothing that Sheffield is. There one seems to be entirely cut
off from the world of 1950 – an impression, by the way, that is
dramatically heightened when one enters beneath the fabulous
gargoyles into the vast church, the largest in Essex, whose
lovely proportions seem designed expressly for those feast-day
pomps and ceremonies that are still performed there much as
they were five hundred years ago. But though Thaxted may

have its "cathedral" and even its charter, it is far more village than town; and rightly the most prominent building, next to the church, is the windmill. So it is, in proportion, with other Essex towns – with all of them, in fact, except the very largest and those of the southern half that are not Essex at all, except in name, but only dormitories for the metropolis.

As for the villages of Essex, they are often set about in scattered groups: the Easters, Good and High; the Rodings, Margaret and Leaden, Aythorpe and Beauchamp, White and Abbess, Berners and High; the 'fields, Bardfield and Finching-field, Toppesfield, Gosfield and Wethersfield; and the Belchamps, Otten, Walter and St Paul. Each has its individuality within the common bond; and each is a little fastness of the genuine Essex character. It is perhaps a foolish pride that singles out any particular village as the best, or even the fifth best, in the land; and anyway, all of these are much to be admired, one way or another; but some such label has been attached to Finchingfield too often for it not to stick. The Essex conservatism, however, is an advantage even here; and perhaps the best thing that can be said about the publicity accorded to Finchingfield is that it seems not to have any ill-effect upon the villagers themselves. If these love their village, with its flint church tower cresting the steep hill, its clustered cottages above the causeway, its ample Green and its air of slow, deep-hearted contentment, this is emphatically not because others have had to tell them how good it is. They still do the right things for the right reasons. The wood smoke rises from the chimneys; the old men, coming from the pub, lean over the bridge for a last-minute argument; and on the Green, where once the donkeys grazed, the village makes holiday. And here, as in other Essex villages, the life and well-being of the place rests, as it should, upon the fields.

But perhaps, after all, it is the hamlets that keep best the essential character of Essex – though they are called Ends or Streets or Greens or, more locally, Uplands, a word that has nothing to do with height but rather with remoteness from the centre. The planners wish to do away with these little outlying communities. It is claimed that they are uneconomic and do not any longer contribute usefully to the general rural well-being; but sometimes I think it is because they breed too strong a sense of individuality for the bureaucrats' peace of mind. Of course, this individuality is not uniformly commendable: the thriftless and the shifty, the misfits and the nohow-fits are cunning at finding for themselves holes and corners where they may escape as much as possible from the clutches of authority, and Essex hamlets are excellent for such. But there also, in thatched cottages clean as new pins, though without water or light laid on and with the most primitive sanitation, live the genuine peasantry, practising their wholesome and simple cottage economy and retaining the very last vestiges of that responsibility towards the land which was once the basis of our agriculture everywhere and in Essex in particular. In them, too, a native wisdom abides, expressed if at all in words that are often akin to poetry; and in their fragile keeping lies all that is left today of our rural crafts and customs. To know Essex, therefore, you must get to know these – if you can still find them.

CHAPTER II

The Place

I. SOIL AND SCENERY

IT is now realised, to an extent that would have surprised our forefathers, that much of the character of a place is determined by its physical features; and one of the first things to understand about Essex, as about any region with which more than a superficial acquaintance is desired, is the nature of its soils. To do this it is not necessary, even if it were possible in this short sketch, to make any deep study of the geological structure of the county; but something at least must be attempted. The use of the land, for example, is very considerably influenced by the nature of the soils – which, by the way, vary in Essex to a surprising extent when its comparatively narrow boundaries are borne in mind. But agriculture is not the only activity thus affected. Architecture, as we shall see later on, is similarly influenced; so is industry and so too is the character of the people themselves.

Leaving out of account such professional and debatable factors as the immense durations of time involved in geological formations, perhaps the best and simplest approach will be to consider the various strata which, when exposed, comprise the surface soils of the county. Underlying almost the entire length and breadth of Essex is a chalk formation (once the bottom of the ocean) of which a considerable outcrop is to be seen in the undulating, and even hilly, north-west corner. Next comes the glacial sand and gravel, visible mostly in the south, by Thanet; and then the famous London clay, extending over almost the whole of the south-eastern district. This is the county's most characteristic soil, being stiff and heavy, impervious to water and therefore needing careful drainage. It is heaviest in the south, becoming medium towards the north-east. Next come the light Bagshot and Reading soils (sand with flints) in isolated outcrops in the south. And lastly there is the boulder clay,

extending north-west from the London clay to the chalk, a clay
which, because of its considerable lime content, is worked more
easily than the London clay, even though it may often be just as
heavy. Thus it will be seen that the various surface soils of
Essex extend as it were in erratic bands across the county, from
north-west to south-east, of chalk, boulder clay, glacial sand,
London clay, and Bagshot sand, the whole sloping gently to the
south-east.

There is nothing typical of Essex in the chalk region of the
north-west: it is a rolling, hilly country of few trees and large
fields. In reality it is part of the chalk belt extending from the
Chilterns to the East Anglian Heights. Almost entirely arable,
its main crop is corn, with a distinguishing predominance of
barley. Sheep are folded on the arable, and, since the soil is dry,
they suffer little from the usual disadvantages accompanying
arable sheep-folding in the Essex claylands. Moving into the
boulder-clay area a difference is at once apparent: corn is still
the predominant crop, but with less barley (except perhaps in
dry years), and the arable is mixed with considerable woodland
and some grassland. The farms are not so large, nor the fields;
and small villages abound. Here the nineteenth-century tradition of corn farming still largely prevails (wheat, barley, and
clover as "cash crops" and roots) with a general disregard for
such crops as need to be sent to a market urgently. The tenor of
rural life here is therefore slow and thorough: there is an
absence of rush which the visitor to its lovely villages, the
Sampfords, the Bardfields, the Bumpsteads, etc., cannot fail to
notice. Further south, but still in the boulder-clay area, are the
Rodings (or Roothings), long famous for their exceptional fertility – a region of wheat, barley, and potatoes, of dense cropping,
and of practically no sheep. South of this, again, is the London-
clay area, hilly, densely wooded, with wide, sprawling hedges, a
notable absence of arable and much grassland, with its accompanying concentration of dairy farmers and poultry farmers and
market gardeners.

Such, roughly, are the main agricultural divisions of the
county, each dependent, as we have seen, upon the nature of the
soils therein exposed. To these, however, must be added various
other divisions, such as the large areas of alluvial soils in the
east – the Essex marshlands – with their great sheep grazings
and little arable; the fruit-growing areas of central Essex (the

gravel soils of the Danbury and Tiptree districts, for instance, and the Tendring region); and the well-known seed-growing area around Kelvedon and Coggeshall, for which the boulder clay, here disintegrating into fine, deep, medium loam, is particularly suitable.

But soils are not the only factor deciding local characteristics. Weather, too, must be taken into consideration. Unkind words have been said and written at one time or another about the Essex climate. Norden, for instance, though he praised the county's fruitfulness, confessed that he could not commend its healthfulness "and especially nere the sea coastes, Rochford, Denge, Tendering hundreds and other lowe places about the creekes, which gave me a moste cruill quarterne fever." And Arthur Young, some two hundred years later, was still complaining about the county's "thick and stinking fogs" and noting with disapproval "the sallow, sickly faces of the inhabitants (near the sea) and the prominent bellies of the children." Such complaints, in fact, were generally limited to the marshlands; but even here, owing to the excellent drainage systems installed in the nineteenth century, they no longer hold good; whilst for the remainder of the county they never have had much application. As for rainfall, only some small areas in the north and west have as much as 25 inches. In fact, a general dryness is one of the county's main characteristics – in spite of the fact that "February fill-dyke" is an Essex saying; but then this refers to the filling of the ditches not by the falling of the rains but by the rising of the springs. Another characteristic is the moderating influence of the sea on the temperature of the county. The general dryness influences the predominant cultivation of corn as opposed to grass, since it provides just the sort of weather essential to the ripening and harvesting of the crop (it is also a decisive factor in seed-growing), whilst the cooling effect of the sea in spring has advantages for the fruit grower by preventing a premature opening of the blossom. As for the effect of the climate on Essex inhabitants, perhaps the worst that can be said is that there seems to be an undue inclination to rheumatism; but this is probably as much due to the cold clay as to the climate and in any case it does not seem to prevent the true Essex native from achieving a ripe old age, longevity in the county surely amounting to something like a record.

If the popular abuse of Essex climate has long since been corrected, a misconception as to its scenic character still persists. "Flat" is the word that immediately springs to mind with most people whenever the county is mentioned; and if its estuaries were the whole of Essex, the epithet would of course be justified. It is true, too, that nowhere does the land rise to more than three hundred and fifty feet above sea-level. But in the country of the blind the one-eyed man is king, and there are modest hills in Essex that command views as extensive as those in many a more hilly county. Danbury Hill, with its view over the Blackwater to the east and the Crouch and Thames to the south, is a case in point; so is Laindon; and so too is Langdon Hill with its unique view to London one way and to Thames-mouth the other. But these have the obvious advantages appertaining to any isolated hill. More characteristic of Essex heights, and much more surprising to the stranger, is the zone of hills terminating the southward spread of the boulder-clay areas – and indeed the quiet undulations of the whole of the north-west of the county. Apart from the estuaries, variety and not flatness is the outstanding feature. And yet wide stretches of open sky are never long absent. I think it is this, the abundance of sky everywhere and the light that pours from it, that after all is Essex's greatest scenic asset. Is there any other county, unless it be Cambridgeshire and the Fenlands, where the sky means quite so much? All Essex men and women are mindful of their light-flooding skies. Let others lift their eyes to the hills: our hope is in the skies. And although of course it is the common practice of all countrymen everywhere to keep a weather-eye on the skies, none search them more consciously, or even more affectionately, than the countrymen of Essex.

II. FLOWERS, BIRDS, TREES

In a county where every available acre is cultivated and where, even before the last war, actual woodland had already dwindled to some five per cent of the area, it would be unreasonable to expect anything very exciting or unusual in the way of wild flowers and animals. What the amount of actual woodland is today there is no available means of knowing, but it must be far below the pre-war five per cent. The war itself took considerable toll when valuable oak and ash woods were grubbed for aerodromes and soft-wood spinneys for pit props; but that was not the end of the mischief. Since the war there have been fellings everywhere, and now an organised onslaught is being made on the hedgerow trees, the excuse being (as if these things should be considered isolatedly and not ecologically) that they waste the ground and interfere with the crops. But my point here is that the whole county is now being cultivated up to the hilt and in consequence wild life of every sort is sadly diminishing. Rich and rare wild-flowers in Essex are therefore hard indeed to find today. Essex used to think itself lucky that it could claim the Fyfield pea *(Lathyrus tuberosus)* as all its own – a variety, so the guide books always boasted, that was only to be found, with its long, trailing stems and trusses of large, crimson flowers, in and near a particular field close to the village of Fyfield, between Ongar and Dunmow. But it would seem that even this modest claim can no longer be substantiated. I have it on the word of no less an authority (though he would be the last to allow the term) than Mr Andrew Young, that it has been seen in Somerset and that it has been recorded in the Sussex *Flora*. Much the same applies to the sulphur clover, which was always said to be peculiar to the county and especially to the Rodings: it is in fact to be found in several of the eastern counties.

If the Fyfield pea and the sulphur clover, however, are so unmindful of their proper station as to stray into Somerset and elsewhere, Essex can always cite Shakespeare's oxlip *(Primula elatior)* not, indeed, as special to the county, but emphatically as more prolific in the north-western district than anywhere else in England today. For me it is the typical flower of Essex and should always be called by its Essex name of the Bardfield oxlip. I know that opinion is sharply divided as to its merits: by partaking of the characteristics of both the cowslip and the primrose, it succeeds, so its critics say, in merely losing the peculiar excellence of either. But I do not agree: the oxlip at its best is altogether a delightful flower. And to see it at its best one should go to any of the woods and copses (where they still remain) in the north-west corner of Essex, particularly around Saffron Walden, where it has its firmest stronghold. Here it will grow to a height of twelve or fourteen inches in the shade, with as many as a dozen flowers to every single cluster, and it fills the April woodlands with its pale light and singular fragrance.

Leave to Gloucestershire its wild daffodils (which, incidentally, were once to be gathered in Essex, in the woods around Quendon and Broomfield and doubtless elsewhere), to Cumberland its butterfly orchises (which the diligent searcher may still find around Saffron Walden and in woods not far from Witham), and to other counties their various floral rarities: the true and conservative son of Essex will be more than content with his Bar'f'll oxlip. Nor will he lightly excuse a certain well-known novelist who, forsaking fiction for fact a while ago, wrote a book on East Anglia, including Essex, in which she mentioned in passing "a variant of the cowslip called five-fingers," airily dismissing it thus: "Five-fingers is of course only the local name; I think the flower is the oxlip"! Of the remaining two primulæ common to the county (the primrose, *P. acaulis,* and the cowslip, *P. veris*) the latter is perhaps even more prolific than the former. Paigles is the local name for it, and I fancy it is to be seen at its best not in the meadows but in the wide grass verges by the roadside. If the natives no longer make cowslip pudding of it (and, since all the petals have first to be snipped away and only these used in the cooking, I could almost doubt whether they ever did – the resultant dish being, as I can vouch, hardly worth all the trouble), or the children cowslip-balls, at least it is pretty enough in the growing – and especially, again, in the Walden district.

The Walden district, in fact, is altogether the best wild-flower centre. Gibson, whose Essex *Flora* still remains the standard work, claims to have found gentians (*G. amarella*) there, and he speaks of the pasque-flower (*Anemone pulsatilla*) as "abundant" in his time in the Bartlow Hills. The pasque-flower does still reward the careful explorer in that district, but of the gentian I cannot speak. I do know, however, that at Widdington, not far away, leopard's bane (*Doronicum plantagineum*) was to be found growing quite liberally before the war and probably still is. There are also lilies-of-the-valley at Bulmer Tye. But on the whole Essex, even in its remoter and more inaccessible parts, is now too exposed to the depredations of the wild-flower vandal, who does not consider his discoveries sufficiently rewarding unless he has plucked out the flower "root and all," to retain many of the rarer kinds, even in this favoured district. Epping Forest too has lost the best of its wild-flower treasures. Here, before it became the Londoners' playground, could be found not only the lily-of-the-valley but also the sundew and the grass-of-parnassus. Many of its ferns have also disappeared: bracken, broad buckler, male fern and adder's tongue being today all that are left from a list that once included the hart's tongue, the polypodies and the mountain shield fern. As much as human vandalism, the intensive land drainage of recent years must be held responsible.

A plant that grows freely in Essex is the spurge laurel (*Daphne laureola*), whose clusters of pale green flowers of subtle fragrance open in January and February and are to be seen in woods and hedges almost anywhere in the claylands. Another hedge plant, especially prolific in the county, is the spindle-berry (*Euonymus europæus*), more noticeable for its vivid display of pink and orange fruit in the autumn than for its diminutive, starry flowers in spring. The wood of this shrub is very hard and was used in the manufacture of spindles and spinning-wheels as early practised in Great Bardfield. Incidentally the powder made from this brilliant berry is reputed to kill nits. Dogwood (*Cornus sanguinea*), once used for the making of lace bobbins, butchers' skewers (because it does not taint the meat), and spokes, is also a feature of the countryside. The vivid red of the saplings in spring led to its being known at Rayne as "bloody sticks" where they were presumed to blush a deeper red at that time of year because of "a foul wayside murder which in 1790 followed Bardfield Fair." Down on the estuaries one of the most characteristic flowers is sea lavender (*Statice limonium*), whose stiff, ribbed stalks bear a pale flower, more sought after for its durability almost throughout the winter when plucked than for any intrinsic beauty: this thrives in quantities between the oozy channels. Sea holly (*Eryngium maritimum*), with its spiny leaves and small blue flowers, is also to be found. Its roots were apparently once very popular as sweetmeats. Indeed, at Colchester they were candied in great quantities both for home and foreign consumption. They were called kissing comfits. "Even as lately as the year 1836," wrote the rather garrulous Ann Pratt, "an immense quantity was sold, in consequence of the inhabitants of Colchester having presented a box of the eryngo roots to one of the Royal Family who passed through the place. ...

Rare wild-flowers may be few in Essex, but the genuine wild-flower lover is not dependent upon these; and he will still find

Essex as prodigal as most other counties in those sudden
surprises which even the humblest wild-flower can spring on the
eye when seen growing to perfection. A roadside bank as white
with violets as if the snow still lurked among the withered bents
of March; a drift of speedwell (*Veronica persica*) on a headland of
arable, blue as the skies themselves and Richard Jefferies'
favourite flower, who told how "the rich blue of the unattainable
flower of the sky drew my soul towards it"; a cleared coppice
that suddenly sprouts with a profusion of hooded windflowers
and shy dog-violets – Essex can match these with any county. It
can even do better than most. I remember one summer day
recently, when a friend and I were looking for a suitable spot to
picnic in. We came at last upon a sign-post pointing down a
lonely, grass-grown cart-way: it read, "To Sibbards Pages." Who
could resist such an invitation? So we turned the car in and
drove as far as the rutty way would let us; and then, rounding a
corner, we were suddenly confronted with a wide verge of sky-
blue flowers – the noontide blue of chicory (*Cichorium intybus*)
massed as I have never seen it anywhere else in England. Later
we came upon some thatched and not too well cared-for
cottages: who could imagine such isolation only fifty or so miles
from London? And beyond these, but still in the grass-grown
cart-way, we spread our rug and picnicked. And when, early in
the afternoon, we finally returned the way we had come and
passed by the verge where the chicory had dazzled us at noon,
there was nothing to be seen but the roadside grass – as if those
thousands of heavenly flowers had been but a dream.

As I suggested earlier in this book, there is, for all its clayey
dourness, a vein of poetry in the Essex character; and so it is
hardly surprising that many of the wild-flowers are still known,
and mainly known, by their folk-names – names by which they
were originally christened when the labouring countryman was
more familiar with nature than he is today, if only because he
was then largely dependent upon wild life for so many of his
salves and simples and herbal cures. One of the features of high
summer in Essex is the greater bindweed that trails its magnificent white trumpet flowers over hedge and flint wall. What
could be more suitable for this cottony white blossom than the
local name of old-man's-night-cap? Most of such folk-names are,
in fact, essentially homely: the greater stitchwort is still called
shirt-buttons, the scabious, pin-cushion, and the scarlet

pimpernel, poor-man's-weather-glass. Flowers that favour arable, from heart's-ease to rest-harrow, are, not unnaturally, among those most readily noticed by the Essex man, and sometimes he will endow them with several names apiece, each being equally popular, as, for instance, the corn crow-foot (*Ranunculus avensis*), which he calls impartially pick-pocket, crow's claw, or simply, joy. These are all more or less understandable; but why, I wonder, does he call ragwort the curse-of-Cromwell?

If, out of fondness and familiarity, the wild-flowers have been given their local names, how much more should we expect a like folk-naming of the wild birds? And so it is: all over Essex the commoner wild birds are known by names that are never heard among the ornithologists. Here are a few of them – and most have by no means yet died out in the remoter districts. Pudding poke, for the long-tailed tit (on account of its nest); butcher-bird, for the redbacked shrike (which impales its food on the thorns of the hedges and bushes); shriek owl and devil bird, for the swift (and what could be more appropriate for this screaming, racing-round-the-houses bird of bad weather?); rainbird, for the green woodpecker; dow, for the dove; old harry, for the curlew; hoverer, for the kestrel hawk (which hangs in quivering suspense as it searches the ground beneath for mice); frank hern, for the heron; hedge betty, for the hedge sparrow; and billy wix (who could *he* have been?) for the owl. All of these are common birds in a county which, with its useful mixture of arable for food and woodland for shelter, is still rich in the commoner wild bird life of England. But as the woods decrease and are not replanted, and as the hedges go down, to enable the farmer to squeeze every penny out of every acre, some of the smaller birds may be driven from their familiar nesting sites, to his and our considerable loss. There are certain districts where the slightly rarer birds may be found. Epping Forest, for instance, by its unique distribution of hornbeams attracts the hawfinch, whilst its plentiful beech-mast attracts that colourful winter resident the brambling. In the few areas where there are conifers the golden-crested wren builds; and the nightingales, though nowhere quite as numerous as in some southern counties where there is more close cover, includes Essex in its well-defined territory.

But of course it is in the marshlands and estuaries and saltings of Essex that the most spectacular wild-bird life is to be

found, whether migrant or resident. From the Essex Thames,
where the reed-warbler nests in the reed-beds that are themselves a marvel (as Sir William Beach Thomas has said), "an
æolian harp in the ears of man and bird," to the Blackwater,
where duck and geese conspire to make a sportsman's paradise,
the water-riddled shore abounds in birds of almost every kind.
Hither, as winter visitors, come the shore-lark and the rock
pippet and the herring gull. Hither (and the harder the winter
the more plentiful) comes the famous brent goose; whilst at all
seasons the black-headed gull and the common gull, the mallard
and the wigeon, are plentiful. But of them all perhaps it is the
brent goose that is most typical of the Essex estuaries, and
many are the stories told in waterside pubs of incredible bags.
There was that February day in 1871, for instance, when
sixteen punters went out together for a flock, firing at it simul-
taneously and at a given signal, with the result that 471 birds
were bagged. It is by such events as these, in the marshlands,
that history is reckoned. Their birds are half the life and attraction of these regions, and two of the islands off the coast of
Essex even owe their names to the immense quantities of birds
that at one time or another have frequented their shores. These
are Foulness Island, north of Southend, and Pewit Island, south
of Harwich. Of the latter, by the way, Fuller somewhat naïvely
reported that "great quantities of pewets are bred here in the
Spring, which, according to the vulgar tradition, come for that
purpose on St George's Day, and sit on their eggs, without
sleeping, till they are hatched. ..."

Duck decoys, where they still exist, are today mainly matters
of curiosity; but there was a time when only Lincolnshire could
boast more than Essex, where in 1800 the number was put at
thirty-two. If they were expensive to keep up, they were nevertheless highly lucrative to their owners. (The one at Tillingham,
incidentally, was the property of the Dean and Chapter of St
Paul's.) There are records of so many pochards having been
taken at Goldhanger, for instance, that they filled a wagon "so
full that the birds in the lower crates were crushed flat."
Londoners, according to Defoe, came down to Essex in numbers
to enjoy a spell of wildfowl shooting; but, he adds, "it must be
remembered that these Gentlemen, who are such lovers of the
Sport, and go so far for it, often return with an Essex ague on
their Backs, which they find a heavier load than the Fowls they

have shot." The art of duck decoying was as complicated as it was efficient, and would seem entirely to merit Mr G. Eland's assertion that "it is a triumph of human ingenuity, celebrated with a silent peacefulness which suggests a Quaker meeting." Silence, in fact, was essential: conversation had to he carried on in a whisper. Even more important was the necessity to prevent any fouling of the scent. According to a Mr Jacob Pattison, who gave a detailed description of duck decoying in the *Field* of Feb. 15, 1868, "some coastguardsmen, cooking a mutton chop in the wind several hundred yards away, once caused the birds to rise from the Tillingham pond; and extra precautions have to be taken in the kitchen of the nearest farmhouse, though quite a quarter of a mile distant, when the wind blows from it to the pond." Even the decoyman, when he had to approach his birds from the windward, held a piece of lighted turf in his mouth.

Another curious art, much practised in Essex in earlier times, was that of hawking. The county was inevitably favoured for the ease with which the king and his courtiers could resort thither and pursue their sport in its plentiful woods and marshlands. Many an Essex estate, in fact, was originally held by the serjeanty of keeping hawks and hounds for the king when he should come hunting, as at Saling, for example, where Ralph Picot held land by the serjeanty of "keeping a sparhawk for the king and mewing it at his own cost," and at White Roding, according to Morant, the manor was held "by the service of keeping two lanner falcons for heron-hawking and a greyhound trained to make a heron rise." Whether a "sparhawk" was as cheap a rental for a manor as might be supposed is doubtful, considering the enormous cost which the tenant incurred every time the king chose to come hunting and hawking.

As for the trees of Essex, strangers are usually as surprised at their number as they are at the amount of hills. Long after the county's general disafforestation, it remained a land of good and plentiful trees. Most parishes could draw on their own timber for the building of houses as well as for the many wooden agricultural vehicles and implements which were in constant demand. Saw-pits abounded; and although these are now mostly tumbledown relics, if they exist at all, there are still some in active use. There is one, for instance, at Seward's End, near Saffron Walden, which Messrs William Moule and Son use for breaking down trees into "flitches and planks"; and, to mention

only one more instance, there is another at Terling, near
Witham. I am indebted to Mr Christopher Reed for some interesting notes on an old saw-mill, no longer in existence, in the
parish of Runwell, in the south of the county; and since there is
a general curiosity about the activities of these pleasant centres
of a minor rural craft, I make no apology for transcribing them
here. Unlike most sawyers, who were notorious for their fondness for taking time off for a drinking bout (and the dust they
endured might almost excuse them), these of Runwell seem to
have been quite exemplary in their behaviour; but then they
were, as we shall see, members of the sect of Peculiar People
who were in some strength in Essex and were held in their
several localities with the greatest respect.

"It was the custom," says Mr Reed, "for wheelwrights to buy
their trees standing: oak, elm, birch, and ash, as a rule. These
they had felled, trimmed, and carted to the saw-pit, where they
would remain until properly seasoned. The local wheelwright
would go along to the saw-pit, select the trees which he wished
to be sawn into planks, and measure up the length required.
The sawyer and his mate had to make a good, clean, even cut at
the base of the tree and again at the top – an important and
skilled job. Then, with a special axe, they squared up the tree
into lengths. When the particular length had been placed on the
sawing frame over the pit, where it was held in position by big,
square staples, one point being tapped into the tree and the
other into a post of the frame, the length was ready for lining
out the planks. If the wood was light coloured, a piece of whipcord well rubbed with charcoal was used; if dark, with chalk. A
line had first to be marked down the centre of the squared tree
for the 'centre cut.' The wheelwright would place himself at the
base of the tree and the sawyer at the top end. When they had
pulled the whipcord taut, the wheelwright would lift it upwards
and let go quickly, the result being a perfectly straight line
down the centre of the tree. They then proceeded to make a
given number of lines, in the same manner, on either side of the
centre cut. The tree was then ready for sawing, the sawyer
standing on top, with his eye on the line, and his mate down in
the pit, getting all the dust. As the sawyer was responsible for
the cleanness of each cut, he was careful to see that the saws
were set to a nicety. Sawyers always worked in pairs, and the
two the writer has in mind were well suited to each other, being

members of a religious society known in Essex as the Peculiar People. On Sunday these people, when attending divine service, which was continuous until sunset, would take at least two meals with them, dinner and tea. All were preachers in turn and all were singers. I do not think the Peculiar People take their food with them these days, but it used to be queer to see basins being kept warm on the stove which heated the chapel. These two sawyers at Runwell were always to be found together: when there was no sawing to be done, they would work in the fields."

Of all the kinds of trees in Essex, pride of place, of course, must be given to the elm – or ellum, as it is locally called. At least, elm is the most numerous tree today, though it was for its oak that the county was famous in earlier times. Oak from Essex woodlands and forests helped to build the great Tudor navies; and much of it is still to be seen, hard as iron and darkened with age and soot, in the cottages, farmhouses and manorhouses everywhere. But elm succeeded oak as arable succeeded forest, for it is a hedge tree; and it certainly shows to best advantage where it stands, immense and isolated, by the roadside verges or on the headlands of the fields. Two kinds predominate, the common elm and the wych elm, and both provide one of spring's happiest auguries when, early in March, their innumerable twigs fatten and are finally tipped with small purple buds that catch the evening light and proclaim, as nothing else, the passing of winter. True, the tree is shallow-rooted ("fleet," as the Essex man says), and therefore it is liable to come down in stormy weather. It also has the unfortunate habit of casting huge boughs, for no apparent reason, on the stillest summer day. And, to complete the list of its shortcomings, it is subject to a disease called the Dutch elm disease, which spreads from tree to tree – though the experts now think they have the upper hand of it. But these unfortunate traits have never succeeded in setting the Essex man's heart against the elm – as it is set against elder, for instance, which he will not burn and will not even allow inside his house, or black poplar, which suffers from the elm's habit of splitting and falling. I am not surprised that Constable, who loved trees as well as clouds and was all but a son of Essex, should have made an old elm-tree trunk, corky and grey-brown and deeply scored, the subject of one of his finest oil studies (Victoria and Albert Museum).

But if the elm is the commonest and most typical of Essex trees, the hornbeam is perhaps its most notable. Admittedly there are better hornbeams in Hatfield Forest; but Epping Forest is nevertheless one of its few English strongholds, and here, grotesquely pollarded, the tree forms one of the features of the place. Being slow in growth, it yields a close-grained timber, harder even than oak and eagerly sought for as the best possible wood for making mill-cogs, plane and pulley blocks, beetles, and all sorts of tool handles. It makes excellent fuel, too, burning, as Evelyn says, "like a candle," and this explains the severe and regular pollarding to which the Forest hornbeams have been subjected. "The special character of the Forest," wrote William Morris, who lived there in his youth and often referred to the place in his writings, "was derived from the fact that by far the greater part was a wood of hornbeams, a tree not common save in Essex and Hertfordshire. ... The said hornbeams were all pollards, being shrouded every four or six years, and were interspersed in many places with holly thickets. Nothing could be more interesting and romantic than the effect of the long poles of the hornbeams rising from the trunks and seen against the mass of the wood behind" – as any traveller on the main Cambridge to London road today will agree. But there are other notable kinds of trees in this six-thousand-acre woodland, and mention must at least be made of its magnificent beeches, its isolated oaks, its crab-apple, beloved by the deer for its sour fruit, and the blackthorn, equally beloved by the birds as a sanctuary.

Ancient trees have always had a peculiar fascination over the minds of men – a fascination which dates back, no doubt, to those pagan days when all nature was considered animate, and trees, no less than human beings, had their souls or "shades." In any case, our primitive forebears were surrounded on all sides by forests, and their little, hard-won clearings must indeed have seemed like kindly islands in a vast and almost impenetrable sea of hostile green. But I have no intention here of pursuing the siren subject of tree-worship. All I wish to observe is that Essex, as becomes a county which was once all forest, has ever shown the greatest solicitude and even affection for ancient trees. Even now there are gnarled old specimens, all but leafless, patched with sheets of lead and tin to keep the weather out of their hollow trunks, that are allowed to stand in the middle of the highway, to the blessed detriment of speeding traffic, for no other reason than that they have achieved immunity by living so long and thereby endearing themselves to the local sentiment. Such a tree is the old oak-tree at Great Yeldham, which still stands today, and of which, as long ago as 1769, Muilman wrote that "the stem measures in circumference twenty-seven and three-quarters feet." He also wrote that it was "supposed to be upwards of three hundred years old." And if anybody knew the truth, this perspicacious old Huguenot should have done so, for he lived nearby and had a most lively concern for such things.

But indeed Essex seems to have treasured more than a usual share of like old trees. Of Fairlop Oak, in the Forest, I shall have something to say later. Another remarkable Forest tree was the "Doodle Oak," as it was called, which (or its predecessor) gave its name to Hatfield Broadoak. Arthur Young, the famous nineteenth-century agriculturalist and reporter on country matters, had quite a passion for such old trees and could never pass one by on his tours without pausing to pay a wordy tribute. Of one, at Hempstead, which was ninety feet high and measured thirty-six yards from north to south (presumably the extent of its widest branches), he reported that "seven waggon-loads of hay have stood under its shelter at one time." I suppose this was the oak-tree which more recently was known as Turpin's Oak (Hempstead being this infamous highwayman's birthplace), but which has now disappeared. Young also wrote of another oak-tree, at Takeley, which he declared was fourteen feet in circumference. But trees attracted him for more than their mere size. He tells of a Lombardy poplar at St Osyth's, for instance, which had been brought from Italy and "from which most of those which are scattered throughout the kingdom originated"; also of an arbutus (the strawberry-tree – a fine specimen of which stands in the gardens of Bridge House in Coggeshall today, bearing each year its fine display of synchronising flower and fruit) at the same place in 1805. It is the more puzzling to me, therefore, that this observant countryman during his Essex perambulations had nothing to say about its innumerable quince-trees, since Essex shared with Kent the most fame for these in the sixteenth and seventeenth centuries. Most old-established gardens in the county and many farmsteads, even today, have their quince-trees beside the pond or moat, growing, as such trees should, with one foot in the water. But quinces have gone out of fashion; even the war, that restored so many forgotten things to favour again, could do no more than give the quince a temporarily renewed lease of life – which seems to me a distinct criticism of the modern palate. Nor have medlars, which are another Essex heritage from the Tudor predilection for splendid retreats and walled gardens in this county, shown any sign of coming into their own again. Of these, the finest I have ever seen was in the forsaken garden of Great Lodge, in Saling, once the stately home of the Lumleys and now fast crumbling away. As medlars are, this one was grafted on to a hawthorn stock; and now, standing beside the reed-filled moat, it presents an unusual sight when in fruit, for the medlars tip every twig and weigh the tree down to the ground, but rising clear of it all is a great crown of crimson haws, proclaiming the inevitable law of the triumph of the wild.

III. FARMING

"East Anglia," Mr A. G. Street has written, "is farming first, last and all the time. Its natives talk farming, think farming and dream farming, knowing full well that in its success lies the well-being of every East Anglian, either in town or rural area." I would not vouch for the truth of this in East Anglia as a whole; but for Essex – which I defiantly include in East Anglia, in spite of the historical fact that, Essex being Saxon and Suffolk being Anglian in origin, the Stour really divides the former county from East Anglia proper – for Essex Mr Street's assessment is valid enough. I am well aware that more than half of its population lives in the London fringe and that the seaside resorts account for a considerable proportion of the rest; but the London fringe, anyway, is Essex in name only and partakes nothing of its essential character. And that essential character is based on farming. Not only do Essex men live mainly on and by the land: it dictates their activities, it monopolises their interests, it even provides the distinctive flavour of much of their speech. It also narrows their outlook and limits their mentality; for it is as nearly true of the average farmer of today as it was of the Tudor farmer in John Earle's day that "he manures his ground well but lets himself lie fallow and untill'd." If you cannot take an intelligent interest in stock and crops, you are a lost man in

Essex; and if you cannot talk of these willingly and almost exclusively, all day and every day, you will soon be reduced to talking to yourself. Similarly, you must be able to appreciate the beauty of a man-made landscape; and to do this requires at least a working knowledge of what goes on "the other side of the hedge." In fact, as far as Essex is concerned, it simply is not true that God made the country: it is man-made to the remotest corner; and your enjoyment of it will depend a great deal on your ability to understand what the process has been.

Indeed, I almost doubt if there is any other county in England where farming traditions have so strong a hold. Other counties may bear the palm for agricultural progress; but Essex beats all for thoroughness. At least it was so, for I hesitate to appear dictatorial today, when all values are in the melting-pot. It always seemed to me typical of the thoroughness of Essex farming that the old-style Essex farmer's walking stick, which he took with him everywhere, was both spade and stick. His eye was on the ground wherever he went, looking for docks and thistles, and with his companionable "spud" he dug them out. Even as he stood talking with friend or neighbour, he would suddenly dart aside to uproot the offensive weed; and on his Sunday walk round the farm, viewing the crops, it was ever busy. Of such a spud, its owner, a grand old Essex farmer, told me this tale: "I've had it twenty years," he said, "and it was given me by the foreman at the Hall here before me. And he had it over forty years. The other day I was walking round the fields and knocked a lump of dirt off a sugar beet with it. Well, it's a thing I've done thousands of times, but this time the spud broke clean in half. I picked it up and walked back to the farm, thinking about old Willy who had given it to me and wondering how old *it* could be and how old *he* must be. When I got up by the Hall, Miss Margery was standing at the door with a letter in her hand. 'Here,' she called, 'I want you. I've just had a letter to say old Willy's dead.'"

Nearly a hundred and fifty years ago, when Arthur Young was Secretary to the first Board of Agriculture, he told enthusiastically how Essex abounded in skilful and accurate ploughmen and how he had just seen a forty-acre stretch "and not a single false furrow." His successor of yesterday –though perhaps not of today – might have said much the same thing. To a certain extent I suppose this thoroughness of husbandry in Essex is due to the fact that the county has always been, and still is, predominantly one of small farms. The same Arthur Young declared, in 1807, that "there never was a greater proportion of small and moderate-sized farms, the property of mere farmers, who retain them in their immediate occupation, than at present"; whilst today, the average size of an Essex farm is only eighty-eight acres – farms of three hundred acres accounting for no more than 6 per cent of the total. Small farms almost invariably imply in their owners a more immediate and personal contact with the fields than can possibly be the case with the owners of large farms. Moreover, it is an attitude which the farmer shares in more or less degree with his employee. Then there is the additional fact that Essex men and women tend to be more than usually tenacious of their birthplace and only reluctantly move beyond the boundaries of their immediate neighbourhood. Certainly this is less so today than it used to be, but it is still a common trait in the Essex character. Such continuity breeds an almost-affection for the fields on the part of the farmhand scarcely less than on the part of the farmer himself. Indeed, affectionate concern for the welfare of the fields is so strong among some of the (particularly older) men that it amounts to a sort of ownership by proxy. See with what close scrutiny, for instance, the villagers will watch his actions when a stranger takes over one of the parish farms. Admittedly much of their criticism (invariably adverse) would seem to be founded on an almost pathological dislike of anything new and untried, whether person or thing; but there is also a very real and outspoken concern lest the fields they have tilled – and their fathers before them – should be in danger of deterioration.

But perhaps the most obvious cause for this agricultural thoroughness in Essex is, after all, the heaviness of the land. Such land, productive of big crops of corn and sheep folded on roots and cattle in the yard, entails by its very nature an intensive cultivation. If you know how to manage the land here, the farmers will say, you can make it grow almost anything. It is a rewarding land; but the reward is only to the hard worker. Drainage is all-important. It has always been a first charge on the Essex farmer, from the days of the primitive but highly effective device of running a straw bond (or even loose straw) in a ditch bottom, which would then be filled in (the straw would then rot, but the drain remained), to the pipe-draining of today.

It is not surprising to find that among the many agricultural inventions of Essex men, whether farmer or labourer, was that of a mole-plough by one Thomas Knight, "an ingenious watch-maker" of Thaxted. Knight must indeed have been an unusual sort of watch-maker except that in his part of the county it is natural for any man, whatever his trade, to take a lively inter-est in the work of the fields; for he also invented and improved many other agricultural implements, including an improved common tumbril, or dung-cart, and a drill.

Indicative of the Essex farmer's concern for the efficient drainage of his land is an amusing incident described in the second volume of the *History of Essex* (1770) by "a Gentleman," the gentleman being one Peter Muilman. "At a parish vestry of Little Yeldham," writes this perspicacious historian, "on the 13th of October last, Peter Muilman Esq acquainted the parishioners that ... all lanes shall be thirty feet wide, the ditches two feet deep ... and the hedges be laid so that the wind and sun may have admittance. ... The said gentleman then observed that persons frequently received alms who were not so infirm but that they might do some little service to the public. ... He proposed therefore that a sufficient quantity of light sticks six feet long with iron scoops about eight inches long and three wide fixed at the ends thereof, be provided by the parish for such poor as receive alms, to be employed in the said lanes and by-ways ... to let out what water may be standing in the roads and to open what drains they may find stopped. ... They should also pick up stones in the horse-paths and foot-ways and lay them in the rutts." One cannot help wondering just what would be the effect if such a proposal were put forward and carried at a parish council meeting today.

Such a county of intensive and thorough farming has inevi-tably bred agricultural reformers and inventors. Not by accident did two of England's foremost agriculturalists, one of the sixteenth and the other of the nineteenth century, spring from this part of the country. Thomas Tusser, whose *Five Hundred Points of Good Husbandry* was for generations the farmers' favourite text-book and the main contentions of which are as applicable today as when they were first woven into homespun rhyme, was born at Rivenhall, in North Essex, and farmed (none too successfully, it appears) "at Katewade in Suffolke," just and only just over the border by Manningtree. The second great agriculturalist was Arthur Young, from whom I have already quoted. It is true that he was born in Suffolk; but he farmed in Essex (also not too successfully) and it was certainly here he gained that intensive training which was to stand him in such good stead when Sir Arthur Sinclair, first President of the first Board of Agriculture, chose him for his right-hand man and gave into his care the difficult task of editing a survey of agricultural England. (Young himself wrote the volumes on Essex and therein provided us with an invaluable picture of the farming life and practices of Essex in the first years of the nineteenth century.)

Both these men, in fact, may be included among the notable men whom Essex bred on its heavy claylands and who in return did much to glorify its name and dignify its state. But they were not the only agriculturalists who contributed more than a local benefit on that ancient and honourable occupation; and since two at least of the others are less known, I propose here to say rather more about them. There was Alderman Mechi, for instance, of Tiptree Farm, down by the coast, who made something like history (and very much like a name for himself) by inventing and installing a mechanical device whereby he could irrigate the whole of his land with liquid manure drawn straight from the cattle-yards. As a result, he claimed to harvest three and even four crops each season of his clover and rye-grass and to rear from four to five pounds' worth of meat per acre annually. Inevitably, since this was in Essex, Mechi met with the strongest opposition and even abuse, being considered by some as nothing better than "a dashing novice in agricultural experience, ready to lavish on his own hasty inventions a fortune acquired in his London warehouse; and all this to make himself famous as a great light in the agricultural world, which light, after all, was a mere will o' the wisp leading its dupes into bogs of bankruptcy." In the nineteenth century, you see, as in the twentieth, London in the eyes of rural Essex was synonymous with all that is untrustworthy and of sharp practice. Nevertheless, Mechi's farm was eagerly visited by farmers and agriculturalists from all over Europe, and there is no doubt he was a pioneer of some importance. A very different sort of innovator was Samuel Jonas, of Chrishall Grange, on the north-western chalklands. Only three of his fields (and he farmed over three thousand acres) were under sixty acres and some were as much as four hundred acres. Jonas believed, in fact, in the greater economical working of big-field farms, and as such was a fore-runner of those who today are urging that land should be laid to land in accordance with the requirements of a mechanised and industrialised agriculture.

Nor would I like to omit from this list of Essex farming worthies the name of Mr Darby of Pleshy. Pleshy nowadays is an attractive little village bordering on the Easters. It is visited occasionally for the sake of its associations with Geoffrey de Mandeville, the earthworks of whose Norman castle are still to be seen there, but otherwise it is allowed to slumber on in unruffled sleep. Pleshy, however, once had its day. One bright summer afternoon in 1886 a marquee might have been seen on Farmer Darby's lawn where a considerable concourse of people had assembled to do him honour. For had he not invented a great Steam Digging Machine which was to regenerate British agriculture? It was Darby's profound conviction that ploughing was all wrong – a conviction by which, incidentally, he fore-stalled by more than half a century the recent American asser-tion, so loudly proclaimed, that "the mouldboard plough which is in use on farms throughout the civilised world is the least satisfactory implement for the preparation of land for the production of crops." What was needed, Darby maintained, was a mechanical digger which, by breaking up the land into small pieces, would expose it to the elements, whose chemical action thereon would be as good as any manure. His first Digger, put together in his own workshop in 1879, had been constructed on pedestrian principles: it walked over the field, in fact, on six feet. But this, he found, would not do: "it jumped too much – had too much of a goose-step about it." And so he proceeded to set the thing on broad wheels, improved and lightened it, and exhibited it at the Carlisle Show, where it was awarded a medal. He claimed for it that it did in an hour as much digging as would require a hundred and seventy men to do, and did it far better. The usual abuse was showered on this worthy pioneer, but it in no way discouraged him; and I have actually talked with one old local farm-hand who remembered seeing the ungainly machine at work in High Easter and had nothing but praise for it. "That dug up a fourteen-acre field on Parson-age Farm," he said, "in two days; and that made wonderful crops."

But if Essex has contributed more than its share of mechanical agricultural inventions and improvements, it is even more remarkable for the tenacity with which it clings to the memory of its old, pre-mechanical husbandry. Even the field-names sometimes recall it. There was a way of ploughing according to the hedge where it followed a curve. This was called rainbow ploughing. It was an exercise of considerable skill; and no doubt the ploughman's pride in accomplishing it accounts, at least in part, for the number of Rainbow Fields that are still so called in various parts of the county. There is one at Stondon Massey, for instance; another at Great Holland; a "Walford's Rainbow" at Finchingfield and a "Rainbow Shot" at Wimbish. In fact, short of the hill counties of England, such as Cumberland and Westmorland, I do not think it is anywhere possible to hear more vivid and circumstantial talk about the old days of flail and sickle, gleaning and horkey and the like. Out in the fields the combine drill will be busy sowing its seed and artificials at the same time; but in the tap-room of the village pub old men will be recalling the skill it needed to do the same job by hand when they were young. With his seedlip (or seedcob) slung against his left side, the sower strode down the furrows, keeping an even pace and scattering the seed with his right hand – each cast made in time with his step. When he had reached the far end of the field he pushed the seedlip round to the other side, and so, returning down the furrows, scattered the seed this time with his left hand. And the old men will boast with pride how they could calculate to within the smallest quantity how much seed they would require for a given area. Or they will tell of the tricky job of broadcasting white clover, and of how one local farmer used to accompany them into the field and spread a big handkerchief on the ground to see how well or ill they were distributing the seed, and of how another farmer, one of the true breed of Essex individualists, always used to sow his own clover seed – on horseback.

Then, again, it is even possible today to come upon some small farmer in the remoter parts of the county threshing out a few seed beans with his flail, this being still the best way of keeping them intact; whilst in the Kelvedon and Coggeshall district it is nothing unusual to see three or four labourers in the field swinging their flails to a lively and regular rhythm as they thresh out the seeds on a spread tarpaulin. Essex even has its own word for the flail, or rather, it has two words: for "flail" invariably becomes "frail" and an older generation use the graphic name of "stick-and-a-half." For an implement so awkward looking it is extraordinary with what nice judgment and easy skill the men use it, and there is no wonder that it and the scythe are invariably chosen as the typical examples in contention of the claim that farmwork in the old days demanded more dexterity and endurance than it does today. The men worked down the threshing floor of the barn (which was sometimes made of oak, sometimes clay and cow dung, sometimes elm boards tongued with iron) swinging their flails as smartly and regularly as a peal of bells. They were so cunning in the use of this clumsy implement that they had no need to stoop to turn the corn as they worked back across the floor but did it with the swingle of the flail – as if the thing were but an extension of their fingers. I have heard it said that in winter one could tell the village threshers by the comparative paleness of their faces, since the work, which might go on throughout the best part of the season, kept them away from the fields; it is also said that one could tell how the men were being paid by the kind of rhythm they kept with their flails – "By the day, by the day!" or, for piece-work, "We took it, we took it!" As for the zest with which old men tell of the task over their leisurely pints today, perhaps this should be set beside Stephen Duck's less enthusiastic account:

> In briny streams our sweat descends apace,
> Drips from our locks, or trickles down our face.
> No intermission in our work we know;
> The noisy threshal must for ever go. ...

Another old farm implement that is occasionally still to be found among the dust and litter of Essex barns and outhouses is the dibble, and indeed most old labourers in the north-west of the county can still remember the day when it was in common use here for the planting of corn. Nowhere else in England was it so generally favoured as in East Anglia, its original home. It was introduced in the eighteenth century, and, although the drill superseded it in the first half of the nineteenth century, it remained in use on many farms in Essex until the 'eighties and 'nineties. The implement is an iron rod about three feet long

with a spade handle at one end and an iron knob, like an elon-
gated egg, at the other. But let an Essex farmer who actually
practised this method of sowing his wheat tell in his own words
how it was done. "A man went backwards with two neat iron
dibbles, one in the right hand, the other in the left, punching
holes in the middle of the flag or turned up earth of every
furrow, about three or four inches deep, and in the line of the
stitches six or eight inches asunder. Two boys followed him, but
with their faces towards his, and consequently going forwards.
They dropped into every hole, two, three, or four grains, as it
might happen; but three was deemed the properest number.
They did about half an acre a day and were allowed ten shillings
an acre. The dibbling being thus finished, a pair of harrows
were drawn up and down the stitches, to fill up the holes with
mould, bury the grain, and complete the work. ..." The dibbles
were given a smart twist from the wrist to firm the holes; and as
for the number of grains deposited therein, a local rhyme puts
the number at five and not three:

> One for the rook
> And one for the crow;
> One to die
> And two to grow.

The dibble created almost as much debate among farmers at the
time as the combine harvester did yesterday, opinion being
more or less equally divided as to its merits. Old men who
actually dibbled wheat seem quite to have enjoyed the job; but
what, one wonders, did the children make of it? I have heard it
said that after filling in the holes all day they were so overcome
with sleep that they had to be carried home in the men's arms.

Nor was the Essex harvest, about which today the older
natives wax so eloquent, nothing but the fun and frolic they too
often would have us suppose. The huge quantities of beer drunk
on the harvest field would seem indeed to be but a measure of
the strenuousness of a task which kept men bending over scythe
or sickle throughout the long stretch of a hot summer's day. And
if there were occasional jollifications and if there was sometimes
a charming display of ritual, had not these things also more
than a hint in them of the need to ameliorate the labourer's
heavy lot? The green bough snatched from the hedge and stuck

on top of the last load of corn; the singing and shouting on the
wagon as it was drawn into the rick-yard; the merry fines of a
gallon of beer or so whenever a harvester pitched his sheaves
badly or when a youngster took his first harvest; and the plentiful food and drink and the rowdy choruses at horkey in the
master's barn – were not these things as much a necessary
oiling of reluctant wheels, without the aid of which the men
could hardly have got through their laborious days, as they were
a sign and symbol of a man's joy and satisfaction in his work? At
least I think it is an attitude that should not be lost sight of.

Nevertheless, there remains, willy-nilly, something nostalgi-
cally attractive about the Essex harvest as it was practised in
those earlier days; and nothing is easier than to fall under the
spell of old men's tales concerning it. Many of the harvest ways
and customs were, of course, common to other counties – and
even to other lands; and so I shall do no more here than to
remind my readers of some that were mainly peculiar to Essex.
"That's the one we've been lookin' for all harvest!" says somebody on the stack as the last sheaf is hoisted up, and it is a joke
without which no Essex harvest would be deemed complete.
Unaccountably, and on the calmest, sunniest day, a miniature
whirlwind will suddenly set all the loose straws in the stubble
swirling in mid-air; and "There's a proper Roger's blast for you,"
says somebody, though neither he nor anybody else could tell
you who Roger may have been. "That's gone to Will's mother's!"
says somebody else derisively eyeing a badly made stack that is
already in need of legs; and Will's mother is with Roger in
limbo. And just as there are (as somebody has computed) a
hundred and twenty different dialect names for the smallest pig
of the litter, of which "cad" and "cosset" are the Essex variants,
so there would seem to be innumerable names for the platform a
stacker leaves at the eaves of his stack to help him build the
top, and the Essex variants here are "gullet hole" and "lazy
man's hole." And finally, to give but one more example of Essex
harvest whimsies, what possible reason can there have been for
the undoubted and widespread popularity of "Who Killed Cock
Robin?" as a horkey chorus?

It was the common practice in Essex to mow the barley with
a scythe and cradle, leave it in the field in rows, turning it from
time to time with a three-pronged barley-fork, and then carry it
loose in the wagon. Of all farm tools and implements I suppose

the scythe has the most willing sentiment attached to it. "Whatever one thinks, or hears said, about a scythe," as George
Bourne wrote, "is agreeable." But then there is an evocative
quality about all farm tackle belonging to pre-mechanical days. I
remember a farm sale one close, thundery day round about
Michaelmas. Everybody was listless with the heat and the bids
had no life in them. Then the auctioneer came to a miscellane-
ous lot which included an old winnowing fan, frayed at the edges
but still lovely and graceful to see – a thing fashioned of man's
hand as light and airy as a leaf. And as it came under the
hammer a murmur and a shy laughing ran through the crowd of
farmers – a gruff recognition of something comely and leisurely
that no longer appertained to farming. But to return to the
"agreeable" scythe. Here, for example, is a note, made at the
time, of a conversation one hot June morning with an old Essex
labourer who was mowing some grass. "'What do you call that?' I
asked, pointing to the wooden pole of his scythe, for I wished to
hear how he pronounced the name of it. 'Snathe,' he replied,
thereby confirming a discovery which had recently been
recounted to me to the effect that, in Essex, the diphthong of the
Old English word 'snaed' does, though rarely, become an ă. This
old man, in frayed and discoloured straw hat, was using a word
that had scarcely changed in a thousand years. ... He then went
on to depreciate the scythe he held in his hands: it was a new
one and riveted. 'My old one was best,' he said; 'but that's got all
wore out. It was a Fussel Mills.' I asked him what he meant by
Fussel Mills. He said he supposed it was the name of the make.
'Another good one was Crown Plate,' he continued, adding that
Halstead was the place most local scythes came from. His chief
complaint against the riveted scythe was that it 'feeds,' by which
he meant that the grass got caught in the nick where the back
curled over and joined the blade – which of course did not
happen with furnace-cast scythes. I asked him if he had ever
heard how the best scythe could be told, namely, by a certain
letter in the groove of the blade, M for Monday, T for Tuesday,
and so on, the least satisfactory scythes being those cast at the
beginning of the week (a Monday's scythe or a Tuesday's), when
the fires were laggard after being let out for the weekend. He
knew nothing of this; but when, later on, we examined his old
scythe (it was hanging, after the immemorial custom, in his
apple-tree – 'that rusts the iron out of 'em') and we found that it

was a Thursday's scythe, the old man was delighted and seemed
to take a renewed liking for the ancient tool, 'wore out' though it
was. ...

Wheat, on the other hand, was cut with a sickle and set up in
the fields in stooks to dry, a process locally known as traving, as
many as fourteen sheaves being placed slanting head to head
across the furrow and pressed close together with a single sheaf
in the furrow at each end of the trave. Nowadays the traves are
usually much smaller and less care is taken in setting them up,
since the whole process of ingathering is quickened and they
may not have to stand in the field so long. Round stacks were
much in favour then and were built not, as now, upon a bottom
of faggots or pea haulm, but upon iron staddles – mushroom-like
contrivances which were supposed to deter the rats from climbing up into the corn. Such staddles, by the way, are still used
every year on the Home Farm at Spain's Hall, in Finchingfield.
A corn stack was indeed "money in the bank" (as the local
phrase goes) in those days, and not a penny must be lost. In
fact, nothing was wasted, which helps to explain the extreme
disgust old labourers exhibit today when they see the straw
being burnt in the field after the combine harvester has been
round: in their time (at least in Essex) the stubble was generally
left standing until after Christmas, as a cover for the partridges,
and then perhaps it was cut and used for the making of lambing
pens or for fuel. Straw was one of the most valuable by-products
on the farm and was put to innumerable uses, both practical
and fanciful.

As there are still flails and dibbles that hide in the cobwebby
corners of old barns, among the bats and owls, to remind us
when we delightedly come upon them of the husbandry of a
more leisurely age, so there are plants that still grow by the
verges and headlands, reminding us of now almost forgotten
Essex crops. These are "escapes": such, for example, as the
teasles that spring up year after year in cart-track and ditch,
the hop bines that aspire from the hedge and twine themselves
up the nearest telephone pole, and the saffron crocus that
surprises in random meadows in the Walden district. Teasles, if
rewarding to the farmer, must have been a tedious crop for the
harvester. They were grown together with coriander and caraway. The coriander, being an annual, yielded a crop the first
year, to be followed the second year·by the caraway and teasle.

The barbed heads of the latter, carefully dried and tied on to poles, each pole a "glean," were taken to the nearest cloth-manufacturer, where they were used in carding, to raise the nap of the cloth to the desired length. Teasles are no longer an Essex crop, but it is still remembered how they were taken through the village by the cartload, one of the county's most curious crops. Another Essex crop which has now passed quite out of cultivation was the hop. This was grown mainly around the Hedinghams, the Colnes, and Halstead, where the Hop Gardens still survive, though council houses may adorn them today instead of the heady bine. Essex hops were grown on poles, for which purpose whole spinneys of chestnut were planted at Castle Hedingham and Finchingfield.

But perhaps the most spectacular old Essex crop was that of the saffron, which thrived in the north-west corner of the county from forgotten times (there is a tradition that it was first intro-duced by a palmer who, returning from the East, concealed a root in his staff), and of which Norden wrote, in 1594, that it was already being grown here in "great store." He also wrote that it "bindeth the laborer to greate travaile and dilligence," which is not surprising when one considers that only the centre of the flower was needed for drying, so that first the petals had all to be stripped away; and for this tedious job, of course, the cheaper labour of women (whose fingers were also more dexter-ous) was used. Most authorities agree it was one of the county's most profitable crops, being much sought after for medicinal and culinary uses; it must also have been one of the loveliest when in flower. Tusser takes it for granted that the north Essex farmer will grow it, at least in small lots, and his equally infor-mative commentator, Hilman, added that after the first crop it made a good sward whereon "Linnen may lye hollow and bleach well enough." Saffron Walden, of course, takes its name from the "flower of the Sun," its original name having been Chipping Walden.

Then there were the Essex vineyards. Controversy is rife today as to exactly what sort of vines were grown here and as to what use the fruit was put. Were the grapes grown for wine or were they merely to he dried for currants? And, if they were grown for the making of wine, why did they fall out of fashion? And why, incidentally, if they throve here once, are they grown so niggardly today even in gardens? One thing only is certain in this controversy: in Essex, as elsewhere in East Anglia, there were vineyards in considerable number. There are records of vineyards at Hedingham, at Debden, and at Great Waltham, to name only three places where the word itself survives in present-day field-names (though it was no more than a pretty guess that ascribed the origin of Radwinter to the "road leading to the vintner's"). As to the varieties of grapes that were cultivated in Essex, the same Hilman specifically states that "if you intend to plant them as in a vineyard" the best kinds for the purpose are "the small black Grape, the white Muscadine, and the Parsley Grape" – and you should "let the Ranks range from East to West." Personally, I think there is little doubt that Essex vineyards produced Essex wine; and indeed, I sometimes wonder whether the cottager's inordinate love of home-made wines, which not even the severe rationing of sugar could substantially curb, may not be traceable to the one-time local prevalence of the vine. Finally, it is not generally realised that tobacco was grown in Essex. By the year 1660, we are told, thirty-one English counties were growing it; and in fact, as we are discovering again today, it is a crop that can be grown on almost any soil, its only disadvantage in this country being the possible lack of sufficient sunshine. Essex had its share of tobacco fields – that is, until the shareholders in the Virginian plantations effected a prohibition in this country. The ban was lifted in 1910, and experiments were once more tried out, though nothing much seems to have come of them here until the present revival of interest in home-grown tobaccos, which is being encouraged by a faithful band of enthusiasts working at Tilty, near Dunmow. Madder was another forgotten crop, though of this I am unable to trace anything circumstantial – unless the reader is interested to hear, in the words of a nineteenth-century agriculturalist, that "so insinuating is the colour property of this plant that animals that feed upon it have their very bones stained of a ruddy hue."

Essex vines, saffron, caraway, teasles and hops, however, are all one now with the flail and sickle, the barley hummeler and the dibble. If I had to name the most discussed Essex crop today (apart, of course, from the eternal corn) I would unhesitatingly name sugar-beet; but I should have to add that, despite the noise it makes and the amount of grousing it invariably occasions everywhere, it is not to be found here in quantity outside the area around Felstead, where there is a beet factory, the Rodings, the border country south of Sudbury, and the chalk hill country of the north-west, since it thrives best on "a good deep soil, rich in lime, potash, and nitrogen." Sugar-beet is a crop of comparatively recent introduction, dating no further back than the 'twenties. It fits in well with the local traditional crop rotation based on corn, taking the place of turnips or mangolds as a clearing crop. But if the farmer likes it for its rich returns, not only in cash but also in animal fodder, the farmhand has nothing good to say for it. So far as he is concerned, it is a nuisance from beginning to end – from, in fact, the day in early spring when he is sent out into the fields to "chop" and single it, row by row, to that other day, in mid-winter, when he finds himself standing in the fog in the same field, his fingers too numb with the cold to feel if they are still there, and his boots barmed up with mud. Even then, when he has clamped it neatly and conveniently by the roadside and secured it against possible frost with a covering of hay or flax haulm or green tops, he has not seen the last of it, for presently, as soon as the factory gives the word or the railway trucks are lined up again in the sidings, it has to be loaded on to the waiting lorries, netted, so that it does not fall off along the road, and driven away. I do not know if it has ever been computed how many tons of our good Essex soil are carted away every year on these endless loads of sugar-beet, to be cleaned off in the washings at the factory and swilled away to the sea, but it must indeed be considerable, and the waste is the worse when one considers that this is all the best top soil. Farmers are encouraged to grow sugar-beet seed and thereby to add yet another novel crop to the lists in Essex husbandry. As for the factory, it can be smelt on a favouring wind for miles around; and, during the "campaign," i.e. the four months during which it is open for working, it provides a focus for converging lorries from far afield and teems with an imported population of workers. When the sugar content has been extracted, the residue is pulped and often returned to the farms as a valuable food for dairy cattle.

Not that the sugar-beet areas of Essex are the best supplied with dairy cattle: these are to be found more in the centre and south of the county – the less intensively cultivated regions. In any case, dairy farming in Essex is not today what it once was. The cheeses, for instance, for which the county was once so

famous do not exist any more. Yet as long ago as *Piers Plowman*
they were a household word in the land; and it will be remembered how, in Skelton's *Rhyming of Elinor Running,* among the
drabs who came to her alehouse was one Margery Milkduck,
whose pledge, since she had no money to pay for her drinks, was
to be –

> A cantel of Essex cheese,
> Was well a foot thick,
> Full of maggots quick:
> It was huge and great,
> And mighty strong meat
> For the devil to eat:
> It was tart and pungete.

Such cheeses came mostly from the marshlands and were highly
spoken of. Norden praised them, long after Skelton, and said
they were "wondred at for their massivenes and thicknes." Yet
by the time Arthur Young came to compile his survey of the
county he could find nothing to say of its cheeses save that "a
good farming cheese" came from the rich pastures of Steeple
Bumpstead and that Canvey Island produced a cheese from the
milk of ewes. In fact, the decline, or something very like it, had
set in long before Young's time. When Hilman came to write his
commentaries on Tusser's *Five Hundred Points,* all he could find
to give voice to in the matter was a typical complaint that,
despite the high standard of Essex dairies in general, the
dairymaids, alas, were not all they should be. "Wenches when
they can get a good Looking Glass, will be running into Places
where they are least suspected, and be combing and tricking
themselves up; and therefore it is not without reason, some neat
Housewives cannot endure a Looking Glass to hang over a
Dresser. ...

Not all Essex, however, is divided between a husbandry
based on corn and roots and one based on dairy cattle: two other
valuable agricultural commodities today are fruit and seeds,
which, if less widespread, are in both cases of the highest quality. Production of seeds is confined more or less to an area
reaching from Marks Tey to Witham; and any traveller on the
main road and rail arteries through the county in summer must
have noticed the vivid fields of flowers, ranging from sweet-peas

to pansies and from larkspurs to sweet williams. Vegetables also are grown for seed here – green peas, runner beans, cabbages, and so forth. The great suitability of the region for seed growing is decided by two factors, the dry climate and the fine, medium loam into which the boulder clay disintegrates. That wisdom is not our monopoly today and will not die with us is evidenced by the fact that the monks of old seem to have been equally well aware of the district's suitability for seed growing: the industry is said to have been started in Coggeshall by the Cistercians. As I have already said, the flail may be seen in action here, threshing out the seeds, and since tractors are really too heavy for the job, much of the cultivation is still done by horses. More extensively practised in Essex is the cultivation of fruit, especially near the coast in the Tiptree area, which is famous the world over for its soft-fruit jams, especially strawberry, and on the Totham Plains. The county even has its own special apple, the D'Arcy Spice, which originated at Tolleshunt D'Arcy and is claimed by connoisseurs of the apple as the best of all keeping "eaters." As an adopted son of Essex and an admirer of this apple I was gratified to read in the Royal Horticultural Society's journal recently that "D'Arcy Spice is in the very first rank, and there is some substance in the claim of Essex folk that it only attains full perfection in their county because it likes a very dry soil. ..." All the same I doubt if, in these days of Cox and nothing but Cox (unless it be shiny and highly coloured but quite tasteless varieties from overseas), it will ever attain popularity. Freedom from frosts, since the Essex fruit-growing districts are steeply sloping and close to the sea, accounts for their concentration here; all the same, the farmers, just to make doubly sure, follow the example of those in the Evesham Vale and have recourse to smoke-pots when the spring frosts threaten to be severe.

It is a sign of the times that these fruit growers should listen to the wireless weather reports to know when to light their pots, having lost the lore whereby their forefathers told the weather without the aid of science. But if Essex farming has progressed a long way in some matters it is still behindhand in others. The Ministry of Agriculture's National Farm Survey of 1947 blandly announced that 40 per cent of the county's holdings had no water supply at all (of the remainder, 26 per cent depended on streams and rivers) and only 35 per cent of the holdings had

electric power available (and of these nearly a quarter drew
their supplies from private sources). And so perhaps it is not
surprising, radio weather reports notwithstanding, if Essex folk
should still on the whole remember and even sometimes act
upon those old agricultural and weather sayings which have
been handed down from generation to generation, nobody knows
how long. There are agricultural words in use in Essex today
that have not changed for centuries – words that you will hear
nowhere else. The haulm of peas and beans, for instance, is still
called "reis," whereby the user unconsciously keeps alive an Old
English word which everywhere else is forgotten. And what
could convey better the action of muck on the land than the
common Essex expression. "That'll *mend* it"?

As for the weather sayings, here are a few which I have not
heard anywhere else. If the cows stand about on the higher
parts of the meadow, it is a sure sign of rain; just as it is equally
a sign of dry weather if the moorhen builds her nest close down
to the water-level. Also: "If the grass grows green in Janiveer,
it'll grow the worse for it all the year." There is even something
approaching a rational basis for such prognostications as these.
Similarly there may be a grain of medical truth buried in the
Essex harvester's assertion that it is unwise to lie in the straw,
face upwards, when you rest after elevenses or fourses or whatever else:

> If you turn your belly to the sky,
> You are sure to lose the following day.

But what, I wonder, can be the basis for the local belief that, if
there are thirteen full moons in a year, the year will certainly be
a wet one? And what about the equally enigmatical insistence
that –

> A Saturday's moon and a Sunday's full
> Never did no good and never 'ull?

Agricultural sayings are, anyway, much more reliable than such
as these. Indeed, they sometimes merely express folk-wise what
the scientist now puts forward as new discoveries. Many of
these sayings, as might be expected in Essex, have to do with
the cultivation of corn. "Sow wheat in the mire and barley in the

fire." "Barley ground ought to be as fine as an ash heap." "Sow
wheat in the slop, heavy at top." "The best muck cart is the
ploughshare." And so forth.

All these sayings date back to the days when the farmhands
of Essex wore smocks, and the horsemen stole extra corn to
keep their horses in good trim, and latten-bells rang in the dark
lanes to tell whose wagon was coming, and the ploughman was
entitled to a harvest-home goose, and the labourers had "seede
cake, Pasties and Furmentie" if the sowing was all over by Good
Friday. They belong, in fact, to the days when the Essex
farmhand, for all that his wages were so low and his lot hard,
yet possessed a sense of responsibility in his work that is now
rarer to find with every passing year. For, make no doubt about
it, the labourer's lot – and perhaps especially the Essex
labourer's lot – was hard indeed. It is not to be wondered at that
he took a foremost share in the several agricultural revolts
culminating in the Rising of 1830, when, like most of the south
and east of England, the Essex countryside was in a state
bordering on insurrection. Ricks were burned, machines were
wrecked. The anonymous letters of "Swing" and his like spread
terror among the starved and almost hysterical labourers, so
many of whom were thrown into prison that the prisons overflowed. With the best intentions, no doubt, but with an unfor-
giveable remoteness from actuality, the village parsons offered
up the prayer as directed by the Archbishop of Canterbury:
"Restore, O Lord, to thy people the quiet enjoyment of the many
and great blessings which we have received from Thy bounty. ..."

IV. ARCHITECTURE

a. Cottage and Farmhouse

If you would discover the local characteristics of any
particular people, you should seek them primarily among the
cottagers. Similarly, if you would see the local characteristics of
any regional architecture, you should look for it in the cottages.
For just as the cottagers live closest to the soil and have, of
necessity and through long generations, framed their habits and
customs, work and play out of their living contact with it, so the
houses in which they live are (or at least were) built from the
materials indigenous to the locality. The characteristic architecture of Essex, in a word, is not to be seen in the mansions of, let

us say, Audley End or Layer Marney Towers, for these were designed out of quite other considerations than economy or accessibility of material. Rather it is to be seen in the thatched and timber-framed cottages of almost any village north of a line drawn from Chelmsford to Bishops Stortford, such as Wethersfield and Pleshey, Wendons Ambo and Little Bardfield, or in the weather-boarded cottages down on the estuaries and marshlands or in certain Forest villages in the south, such as Lambourne End. These cottages, whether of wood or plaster, suit the surrounding landscape – grow from it, one might say – because they are built with local material and because they have been designed, in a dozen ingenious and attractive ways, to withstand the prevailing weather in their district; whereas the mansions may almost be said to create their own landscape and would, as often as not, look as well in the wet and pastoral West Country as here in the dry and windy east.

To a certain extent, admittedly, the farmhouse must share with the cottage this commendable feature of local suitability of character, since it too is composed out of local material and designed no less to combat the local climate. Nevertheless there is a difference. A farmhouse is only in part a house for living in: it is also a practical adjunct to the farm itself; and its design, which must of necessity be at least partly conditioned by this fact, shares therefore a common factor with other farmhouses all over the kingdom. In a cottage, on the other hand, the design is conditioned by nothing but the bare simplicities of the cottager's daily domestic life and so is that much the more typical of the people who live in it and of the place where they live. Gradually, of course, these old cottages are being dwarfed and outnumbered by newer cottages, which at their worst flaunt the ignorant and unholy intentions of the jobbing builder and the flagrant exploiter, or at their best reveal the standardising tendencies of the age. The most obvious examples of the latter are the council houses; and it has to be admitted that these and their like are apparently what the countryman (but especially the countrywoman) increasingly prefers and clamours for. It is true that the attraction wears a little thin once the cottager moves in and begins to taste the sweets of officialdom – the "do this" and "don't do that" with which he soon finds himself hedged at every turn; but even so I see no signs yet of a drift back to the old thatched and half-timbered cottages.

Nobody could reasonably accuse the Essex native of wearing his heart on his sleeve: his tendency, in fact, is to keep it so strictly out of sight, behind the harsh homespun of his exterior nature, that the stranger and the newcomer might almost suppose he had no heart at all. And it is much the same with the traditional Essex cottage and farmhouse: their most attractive feature, namely, the old oak beams and studs, are all inside; and even then they are often concealed from sight beneath a coat of whitewash or a dozen or so layers of unlovely wallpaper. (It is customary to pour scorn on our forefathers for the bad taste they showed in whitewashing their good oak timbers; but there is at least this to be said in their favour, that smoke-blackened beams on wall and ceiling would have added considerably to the gloom of any small-roomed and small-windowed cottage in the days before electric light or even incandescent oil-lamps.) Nor should the wooden frames of these old houses be exposed to view, as many in recent years have learned to their cost. The builders knew very well what they were about when they encased the oak studs in a good, thick coating of lath-and-plaster or filled them in with a substantial packing of wattle-and-daub. A better non-conductor they could not have devised. To provide warmth and shelter from the bitter east winds that prevail in these parts was their aim, and magnificently they achieved it; nothing could be cosier than a timber-framed house that has not been tampered with by ambitious but foolish owners who are out to catch the eye and find, instead, that they have merely caught a cold. And when to filled-in plaster walls is added a roof of thatch eighteen inches to two feet thick, cool in summer and warm in winter, the lover of comfort could hardly wish for anything better. I remember reading an excellent piece of advice to intending purchasers and renovators of old cottages. "You will probably find an earth closet down the bottom of the garden: leave it there." And to this I would add the recommendation (born out of due experience) that if you are lucky enough to live in an old Essex home whose timbers are encased in lath-and-plaster, you would do well to ponder the obvious truth that it is better to look plain and feel warm in winter than it is to look beautiful and freeze. And with regard to the construction of this old-time filling of lath-and-plaster, a word here may not be out of place. Split saplings of ash, or hazel were sprung into grooves made in the upper and

lower horizontal beams, whilst shorter crosspieces were wedged
between the uprights. Clay, mixed with chalk and chopped
straw, was then worked in between the wood until the whole
lattice of laths was thus covered with a rough-daub cement.
Examples of this may still be seen in any old house where the
renovator's zeal has not been allowed to outrun native wisdom. I
remember visiting an Essex farmhouse recently where, the
snow having come through, some structural alterations were in
progress. Slabs of this roughly "cemented" lath-and-plaster lay
about the yard. They were so heavy I could hardly lift them. The
farmhouse was a moated one (as is so often the case in this
county), and I dare say the clay which was used in making the
house had been that which was dug out to make the moat. In
addition to the hazel laths, I noticed that honeysuckle bines had
been worked into the mixture, and they were as strong and
intact as when they were cut from the bushes some four to five
hundred years ago.

It must have needed much skill and no little ingenuity to
construct these old timber-framed houses – and especially the
more considerably sized farmhouses. How was it done? The
usual contention is that the wood, after it had been carefully
sorted out and shaped with the adze, was laid in place on the
ground in the builder's yard, where it was chiselled with rough,
distinctive markings so as to facilitate matters when it was
finally ready to be removed to the actual site chosen for its
erection. (It is not unusual to come across such markings today
on the studs and uprights of old half-timbered cottages and
farmhouses. Sometimes these markings are merely Roman
numerals, but others suggest that each Essex builder had his
own curious system of jointing marks.) But whatever may have
been the actual method of construction, the fact remains that
those early builders – who, it should be remembered, had only
an adze with which to smooth their timbers and used only
wooden pegs to secure the joints – achieved a construction
which is every bit as comely as that which their West Country
brothers achieved when working in the more malleable limestone. Many such old Essex cottages and farmhouses, which
have already stood for four or five hundred years, are as serv-
iceable today as ever they were. And if some of them now seem
to lean rather precariously, so that the floorboards slant at most
inconvenient angles, this is only because the building has

"settled" this way on the yielding clay of its foundations. By comparison, one has only to ask oneself what will be the condition, even after half a century, of some of the houses which are being put up today, whose timber is so unseasoned that the delighted tenant has scarcely moved in when gaps begin to appear all over the place and fixtures to jump out of joint overnight?

Nothing in the builder's craft so plainly betrays the difference of outlook and attitude between ourselves and our forefathers as does their conception of ornament in architecture. Usefulness was always their first consideration, and such ornamentation as they admitted in their building was based solely on this; yet who could say that the result is less attractive than the modern conception of decoration for its own sake? One of the features of Essex plaster-work is its pargetting – the local name given to that relief sculpture, sometimes highly complex, sometimes confined to one simple repeated figure, which may be seen, if only today in fragments, all over the county. Admittedly some of the finest examples are to be found just over the border, as at Clare, where the pargetting on a house beside the church achieves almost fantastic proportions; but the pargetting on Colneford House at Earls Colne and on the ancient "Sun" house at Saffron Walden, to name only two instances this side of the border, would be hard to beat, whilst minor examples, such as certain fragments surviving in Cornish Hall End and Wivenhoe and elsewhere, suffice to show the original Essex cunning in this forgotten art. But pargetting, however lovely the result may be, was primarily intended to be of use in the general structure of the house: by breaking the fall of the rain as it ran down the sides of the house and over the surface of the walls generally, it helped to prevent the plaster from disintegrating. Such complicated examples as I have just mentioned are mainly to be found on the bigger houses – farmhouses and converted manor-houses; on cottage walls the pargetting was usually of a very simple nature, one favourite device, repeated all over the exposed surfaces, consisting of a stylised cockle-shell, said to have been based on the emblem worn in medieval times as a badge of service in the Crusades. Nor was pargetting the only architectural decoration which had its origin in utility. Even the apparently fanciful arrangement of the ledgers and spics (twisted hazel pegs, for securing the thatch) was intended, though the

thatcher of today has quite forgotten the fact and now for the
most part contents himself (and saves time) with a single line of
them at ridge and eaves, to strengthen the thatch at its most
vulnerable places and so enable it to withstand better the stress
of inclement weather. And barge-boarding, which is the
builder's name for those frilled and fretted boards which are
sometimes to be seen at the open end of the roof, had a similarly
protective purpose for its origin. In fact, almost the only purely
decorative work on these old thatch and plaster houses is the
colour wash with which they are painted. The usual colour is
either white (which offers a most effective background for the
play of shadow-boughs from any tree near the house) or cream.
But terra-cotta is a traditional Essex colour wash for cottages,
too; and to my mind nothing could look better than this when it
occurs, as at Rickling Green, on thatched cottages tumbled
round the village green.

There is a cottage and farmhouse style of architecture, later
in date than timber-frame and plaster, but preceding the present standardised building, which by no means gets the attention
it deserves. I am referring to the brick-and-flint inlaid house
(especially of the cottage type) which sprang up in the north
Essex villages during the nineteenth century. In matters architectural it is the fashion today to turn a blind eye to anything
later than the eighteenth century; but such an attitude is at
best sentimental and at worst downright snobbish. The nineteenth century, in whatever other way it may have offended
against the canons of good taste, did at least witness a considerable amount of pioneering work in the designing and building of
cottages – especially of labourers' cottages and farm-buildings,
as may be seen from the copious plans which appear in the
agricultural manuals and encyclopædias of the time. Many a
nineteenth-century squire braided his own posthumous laurels
by the act of erecting on his estate farmhands' cottages which
were as novel and progressive in their own day as they are
admirable (if we were not blinded by prejudice) in our own.
Sometimes, admittedly, he made concessions to the whimsical
fashion of his age by giving them a superficial resemblance to
the Gothic. Sometimes, too, he emphasised his unconscious
pride in ownership by affixing his monogram, neatly framed,
over the cottage doorways or under the eaves. On the whole,
however, he is to be commended for his additions to village

architecture and even to be praised for the readiness with which he admitted the several innovations of his architects.

One of the nineteenth-century Essex cottage styles which I personally like best is the brick-and-flint style – the general structure being of flint (or cobble) with strengthening and ornamental courses of brick. Brick, though greatly in favour with the builders of Tudor mansions in this county, is very rarely to be found as a basic building material for early cottages and farmhouses: in these the only brickwork as a rule is the chimney-stack. The bigger, clumsier bricks of the nineteenth century, though still considered too expensive for the majority of cottages, were nevertheless used to give a supporting framework to the less tractable flint or cobble, much as imported stone was used (as we shall see presently) to strengthen the native flint towers of many Essex churches. Cobbles give a homely look to a place. They have less of the sharp, light-reflecting surfaces that lend such colour and variety to flint, yet they are not without their own quiet attraction. The art of building with these, as with flint, has all but died out now, so that it is impossible to find anybody capable of mending even a flint wall satisfactorily, let alone building one. Even the old cobble paths that used to lead up to the cottage door, gleaming in the rain and modestly shining in the sun, have for the most part been buried deep beneath layers of ashes and cinders, or, more possibly, pulled out altogether. A word should he said, too, of the familiar Essex custom of building a flint-and-brick wash-house just outside the back door. Only on Monday morning, of course, do these comely adjuncts to the cottage group come alive, with smoke from their chimneys and billowing clouds of steam from their doors; but at all times the copper comes in handy for other things than the week's wash. If, for the most part, the wash'us still stands and is used, the bake-house is now little more than a memory. Where a whole row of cottages was concerned, the bak'us was likely to be a communal affair – to the considerable detriment of good neighbourliness. Sometimes it was merely a brick-built oven beside the chimney, fed from indoors, the oven proper being visible outside in the shape of a clay-covered dome. In either case, the technique was the same. Faggots or hedge trimmings were burned in it, and the cottager could tell when her oven was hot enough for baking by the ingenious device of a quartzite pebble (called the oven watch)

which was built into the back wall of the oven. When this
glowed, she knew that the oven was at baking heat, and now the
ash could be raked out and the loaves slid in on the long wooden
peel. Baking day was about once a fortnight in winter and
rather more frequently in summer, when the bread did not keep
so well. Incidentally, one attractive feature of these ovens,
where the entrance was from the cottage hearth, was their iron
doors, which were often beautifully worked by the local smith.

b. Mansion and Manor-house

No other county has a richer or more delightfully varied
assortment of Tudor mansions than Essex. Nearness to the
capital, together with unusually good opportunities for the
pursuit of such sports as hunting, hawking, shooting, and the
like, rendered the county peculiarly attractive to those Tudor
noblemen whose time was so nicely divided between court and
country. Royalty favoured Essex a good deal – especially Henry
VIII, who partly built and sometimes resided in the sumptuous
New Hall at Boreham (now greatly reduced and occupied as a
religious house), and who, if persistent legend is to be believed,
housed more than one of his mistresses in the county, as at
Shenfield and at Newland House (now dwindled to a farmhouse)
and again at Jericho House, which earned its name, apparently,
because inquiries as to the king's whereabouts were all too
liable to be countered with the discreet "He's gone to Jericho!"
And truly the Tudors choose well. In addition to the attraction
of hunting and shooting and hawking (and was not the first
treatise on hawking written by an Essex noblewoman, Dame
Juliana Berners, of Berners Roding – one of the first books to be
printed in England) there was the dry, sunny climate, which
enabled them to give full scope to their newly acquired and
intensive love of gardens, so that, with the aid of a walled
garden, they could produce almost anything from peaches to the
finest grapes, from quinces to the new-fangled "salats." They
also built their houses with rare good taste, stinting nothing in
the endeavour to outdo the similar efforts of their neighbours –
yet it was not done so much in ostentation as in a fine, inventive
grasp of what constituted good architecture. Admittedly there
was ostentation, as at Audley End, which owed its name and its
former magnificence to the powerful Chancellor Thomas Audley
in the reign of Henry VIII. What remains today is magnificent

enough, and lovely too; but it is only a shadow of its former self. Perhaps the best view of it is from the main Cambridge to Bishops Stortford road. A ha-ha on either side of the highway gives the traveller an uninterrupted view. The silver Cam slides gently through the level meadows whose great trees sweep the flower-filled grasses. By one of the entrances stands the Stables, as fair an example of Tudor brickwork as any I know. It is exceptional to go that way and not see an artist sitting somewhere nearby trying to capture its elusive charm on canvas. Audley End was always a favourite with royalty. Even Charles II took a fancy to the place, and acquired it but failed to pay for it. There is a local legend to the effect that while Catharine of Braganza was in residence, she slipped away one day with some of her ladies and, disguised in country habit, visited the Walden fair and bought at one of the booths "yellow stockings and long gloves stitched with blue"; but her foreign accent gave her away and she was all but mobbed by the delighted yokels.

Another spectacular Tudor mansion, which has now disappeared altogether, was Wanstead. It was the Earl of Leicester's great country seat, where he so lavishly entertained his queen and such famous fellow courtiers as Sir Philip Sidney. The mansion, it is amusing to note, included, according to Muilman, "a neat building, furnished with stove and artificial places for heat, from an apartment which has a bagnio, and other conveniences both for use and pleasure." Nothing remains now but a memory: Wanstead belongs to the lost Essex of the south. Then there was New Hall, at Boreham, already mentioned, a Tudor mansion which in its time was second to few. It was occupied successively by such illustrious personages as Henry VIII, Queen Mary, and Queen Elizabeth, Villiers Duke of Buckingham, Oliver Cromwell, and General Monk, of the latter of whom Muilman wrote that he was "the happy instrument of restoring monarchy to its wonted splendour and checking the increasing of democratic government. ... He lived at New Hall in the utmost pomp and grandeur, having everything that wealth could provide or fancy invent."

The more modest Essex mansions were for the most part built of brick – a strange anomaly, one might suppose, in a county where wood is the obvious material. But bricks were made in Essex as far back as the thirteenth century, although their plentiful use later on was due to quite another reason. But let me quote here the excellent authority of Mr Hugh Braun. "During the fourteenth century," writes this knowledgable historian of the English house, "the export of wool from this country to the Continent was increasing to a considerable scale, so much so, in fact, that the European countries were unable to export to England enough commodities to keep a trade balance. The result was that most of the foreign ships, especially those coming from countries which did not produce wine (England's chief medieval import) were forced to come over to our ports in ballast. Bricks made an excellent ballast, and could at least be got rid of at a price instead of being merely tipped out at the harbour mouth. So bricks it was – and we may be very thankful. The architecture of this country might have been so much the poorer without the fine East Anglian brick buildings of the days of the Tudors." Even the lovely Cotswold limestone was scarcely more congenial to the masons who worked in it than was the Tudor brick to the builders of Essex. Being thinner than the modern brick, it gave a more delicate texture to the surface of the wall; and moreover, being baked in fire, it added the glow of a more various and subtle colouring. For ornament there was often a moulded string-course, or curvilinear gables might be added after the Dutch fashion, as at Spain's Hall in Finchingfield, where the still older main building has been given a brick façade whose curvilinear gables and stone-mullioned windows offer a most pleasing prospect, whilst the whole surface, when the evening sun shines over it, glows with an inviting warmth; or the bricks might even be worked into simple patterns by the use of black bricks, as at Layer Marney Towers, or set in herring-bone fashion between the oak studs, as at Monks Barn, in Newport, and elsewhere, to the great enhancement of the whole building.

The English way of laying the bricks – English bond, as it is called – was to build with alternate layers of "headers" and "stretchers," thereby showing either all ends or all sides; but later, in the eighteenth century, the Flemish bond was adopted over here, whereby "headers" and "stretchers" were laid alternately in every row of bricks – a scrap of information, by the way, which may be applied with some degree of reliability where the date of a house, or of part of it, is unknown. It would be useless here to attempt to name all the fine examples of brick-built Tudor mansions in Essex: the best thing seems to be to give my personal choice of a few which I, anyway, find of special appeal. These are Horeham Hall; Faulkbourne Hall, with its fine tower and lovely prospect from the well-wooded park; Gosfield Hall, with its great courtyard, one of the county's most imposing mansions, now, alas, sharing the fate of so many others up and down the land; Layer Marney Towers, which is in fact not a mansion at all but only the enormous gateway to the projected and never completed house; Rickling Hall; the previously mentioned Spain's Hall, smaller than most, but perhaps the more intimately beautiful for that, and bearing still the comfortable look of a house that has been continuously occupied for centuries; and Panfield Old Hall, with its fine clustered chimneys and its quadrangular towers. Such chimneys, it should be added, are a feature of Essex houses. There are examples everywhere, particularly of note being those at St Osyth, at Radwinter (Grange Farm), at Newport (Martin's Farm), and at Helion's Bumpstead. Here the chimneys, all based on a central flu and each following its own original design (the most popular, perhaps, being the spiral), form an ornamental cluster that is the crown and glory of the house. Another feature of such old mansions was the use of secular mural decorations on the walls of the living-rooms, which are more common in Essex than anywhere else. Campions, at Sewards End, was a good example of this domestic refinement in earlier days, and there are several specimens still to be seen in the excellent museum at Saffron Walden.

And what will happen to these grand old Tudor mansions? All but servantless today, unoccupied except for a bare minimum of rooms, their valuable libraries and pictures and furniture deteriorating for lack of heating facilities, their parks, as likely as not, ploughed up for crops, their fine old trees felled to pay debts – they present a problem which is the general public's almost as much as the harrassed owner's, for they are among the chief ornaments of our lovely countryside and a poignant reminder of the English genius for domestic architecture in the years gone by. Gosfield Hall is an outstanding case in point. History is in every room of its great quadrangle. Recently it was sold up, and a most affecting experience it was to ramble through the beautiful but denuded rooms (including the oak-panelled gallery, one hundred and six feet long, called after Queen Elizabeth, who twice visited Lady Maltravers here on her splendid progresses). From the windows one looked out over the great parkland, with its wide sheet of water, one of the finest in the county and the resort, with every hard frost, of all the skaters in the district. But then Gosfield Park was always a popular resort for Essex people, as witness this ingenuous description from the easy pen of the author of *The People's History of Essex* (1861): "On the north side, after passing upon the lawn Baily's statues of 'The Maiden preparing for the Bath' and 'The Tired Huntsman,' we entered a thickly wooded tract, broken up, however, by long green walks and pleasant glades and opening vistas. ... In the midst of this sylvan scene we found the bricked sides and furnace of an unromantic looking copper. On inquiring what this meant, we learned that on the Sunday afternoons of summer, and on other occasions, these grounds are thrown open to the public, when they are frequented by hundreds, who, drawing their sober supplies from this copper, range themselves in parties on the rustic seats formed of prostrate fir-trees, placed purposely by the walk sides, and enjoy the friendly cup and the fresh free air."

A manor-house, if we are to abide by definitions, is a house, usually fortified, in which lived the feudal lord of the manor. But already by Tudor times it was no longer fortified and the lord had lost most of his rights. And today it may be only a farmhouse. Indeed, there is many an Essex farmhouse which (if the farmer, immersed in his sole concern with stock and crops, were interested in such things) has quite as long and eventful a history as the mansion on whose estate it stands. A farmhouse called Claverings, near Stisted, is surrounded by a complete moat – or "motte," as the natives rightly call it. It is, in fact, the only completely moated farmhouse I know of in Essex, rich as this county is in these originally defensive waterways. And what chapters of unrecorded history, I wonder, does this portend? Tiptofts, at Wimbish, is even more remarkable. The earliest portions of this remote old farmhouse actually date back as far as the year 1300. It has an aisled hall which is unique and a rectangular moat which is associated in local legend with the notorious Essex highwayman Dick Turpin, who was born at Hempstead not far away and whose horse, Black Bess, is supposed to have leapt over it on one of her master's nefarious escapades. But the most unique thing about Tiptofts, after all, is its name. As we shall see later on, Essex place-names are alto-

gether remarkable for the history they reveal, but few are more
remarkable than Tiptofts, which is the name of its first owner,
John Tippetoft, who appears in the Feudal Aids of 1346, having
married at this date the lady who brought him the manor. Thus
for six centuries, through all vicissitudes and changes of ownership, this lonely old house has remembered its original master.
In short, one never knows what story there may be hidden
behind the workaday exterior of an old Essex farmhouse. Even
its outbuildings sometimes are historical. At Latton, for example, there is a barn which was once part of a priory; and at
Wicken Bonant a former chapel-at-ease was until recently a
cowshed and even now is used for housing grain.

But of all Essex manor-houses with long and honourable
histories, the one which has the longest and most honourable of
them all is surely Temple Cressing, about which sheer enthusiasm, if nothing else, would compel me to write at some length.
Here are no ruins, no abuse of ancient buildings: its present
owner is as mindful of the rich heritage of the past as he is
concerned to keep pace with the demands of to-day. What
immediately strikes one on entering the gateway into the drive
is the mellowness, the ripeness of the entire group of buildings,
from the house itself to the cattle- yard and outbuildings and
two enormous barns close by. They all seem to grow together –
like the leaves and flowers of a single plant. And well may they
wear a mellow look; for here, in the twelfth century, the Knights
Templars, most charitable of Crusaders, had one of their several
perceptories; and when, a couple of centuries later, they were
evicted and deprived of their property, it was handed over to the
Knights Hospitallers of St John of Jerusalem. Two more centuries and these also were evicted, and thereafter the manor
passed into private hands. But the history of Temple Cressing
goes back even further than this. Heaped on table and floor in
the present estate office are hundreds of shards. They are bits of
Roman pottery: some are of still earlier date. All were dug up
here in the fields around the house – evidence of Roman occupation. Indeed, the centuries here mingle and overlap: it is almost
impossible to come to the place and not be aware, somehow, of
its immemorial continuity of activity. House, barn, granary,
stables, gardens, moat, and paddocks – the whole pile
proclaims, if not in so many words, that this fair corner of Essex
is holy ground. But it is the two barns, if only by their size, that

attract most attention. The tithe barn of Great Coxwell, in the West Country, is usually acclaimed as the finest in England; but I for one, and not merely out of regional patriotism, would give the palm to these two great barns of Temple Cressing, the one for housing barley and the other for wheat. They are of oak, so hard a nail will scarcely pierce them, and carrying in every king- and queen-post, every tie beam and pillar more than a suggestion still of the trees when they were growing. One, the Barley Barn, which dates back to 1480, has an attractive display of brick- nogging between its uprights; but the chief feature of both of them, after all, is the immense span of their roofs, sweeping down in gentle curve from the ridge to the low eaves, acres of tiles (78,000, weighing 74 tons, on each barn) pitched up against the sky. Temple Cressing wears its history like an aura. Here, one cannot help feeling, is Old England revealing herself, in shy hint and sudden gleam, to all who have an eye to see and a heart to understand.

c. *Church and Castle*

Not surprisingly, there are very few stone churches in Essex. The commonest building material is either brick or flint or a combination of both, or pudding-stone, a conglomerate obtained from the chalk and gravel. Where there are stone churches it is because they were the gift of donors whose wealth was sufficiently vast to enable them to bear the heavy expense of transportation in those early days, or else, as in the case of a number of churches down by the Thames and the Crouch valley, the site was near enough to stone quarries to render its use economical. The ragstone of the churches in these last-named regions comes, of course, from over the river, in Kent; transportation by water, therefore, would have been neither too difficult nor too costly – though it must be admitted that Wealdstone church, which has a Tudor tower (all that remains of the original church) built entirely of ragstone, is a fair distance inland. The remaining chief exceptions to the Essex rule of brick and flint are her major churches, such as Saffron Walden or Thaxted. The latter, which is the largest and I would say far and away the loveliest church in the county, is mainly built of clunch stone – a soft limestone of which the worst feature is that it weathers badly, so that such exterior sculpture as survived the iconoclasts and vandals has hardly survived the wind and rain. It is a fine

example of the Early Perpendicular style (though by no means
all built at the same time), just as Walden is a fine example of
the Late Perpendicular. Together, these magnificent churches
are the chief glory of Essex ecclesiastical building (if one except
the remains of the one-time splendid Waltham Abbey) and far
outshine the cathedral of the county town of Chelmsford.

Thaxted church, in fact, is usually described as the Cathedral of Essex and may even originally have been so intended. It
stands on the crest of the hill and its tremendous spire (one
hundred and eighty feet – nearly twice the height of Walden's) is
a landmark for many miles around. As the 'buses speed along
the narrow roads that converge on the town, between the cornfields, suddenly one sees the lofty spire pointing up through the
trees; and somebody is sure to say "There it is!" as if this were
the moment he always waited for on the journey home. And
there is no doubt Thaxted folk do love their church and are
proud of it, as well they may be, not only because it is so beautiful in itself, but also because it is so alive in spirit. So alive –
and yet perhaps that is the last description anybody would
apply to the little town that appears to be so very remote from
the nervous, hurrying, machine age of today. But Thaxted was
not always quiet and sleepy. Back in the Middle Ages it was
famous for its wool trade, and even more for its cutlery trade.
(One of the hamlets outside the town is still called Cutlers'
Green.) It was during this period of prosperity that the church
was built; or, rather, work on it was begun then, for all told the
building of it took more than a hundred and fifty years. It is
essentially the church of a wealthy trading community, like the
"wool churches" of Suffolk and Norfolk, though the great town it
was meant to serve has shrunk now to a village.

I suppose the first thing most people notice on approaching
the church is its gargoyles, as fantastic a collection of nightmare
creatures as can possibly be imagined. One of these, however,
represents a man howling with toothache: the poor fellow has a
big bandage tied round his face and leans forward in obvious
pain. In addition to the gargoyles there are carved animals and
flowers, a rabbit sitting up, a sleepy deer, a boss of lovely foli-
age. Hidden away in the outside west wall of the church, down
among the grasses behind the altar, is a memorial tablet to
Conrad Noel, who, as Vicar of Thaxted (and I believe a descen-
dant of one of the church's original founders), did more than

anyone else to give the place its vivid character. "He loved
justice and hated oppression," the inscription reads: good words
for a good man. Immediately upon entering one is seized with
admiration for the lightness, the airiness, the spaciousness of
the building. As at Walden, the windows are mostly of plain
glass, the original stained glass having been nearly all
destroyed; and instead of dark pews crowded about narrow
aisles, there are chairs in the nave, which can be added to or
taken away according to the size of the congregation. All this
makes for a delightful absence of stuffiness: there is a sense of
out-of-doors, which is further emphasised by the many taste-
fully arranged pots and bowls of flowers all over the place. As
for colour, some at least of what was lost from the stained
glass windows and the painted roof has been replaced by the
galaxy of hanging banners in the chancel and the bright stuffs
here, there, and everywhere; not to mention the blaze of colour
from cope and candle, cross and swinging censer on festival
occasions.

If the remainder of the Essex churches are, in the matter of
sheer magnificence, no match for such as Thaxted, they nevertheless have a great deal of charm, especially in the villages.
More than usually, I think, they may be said to "belong" to their
landscape – as Constable realised when, in so many of his
pictures, he made the great flint tower of Dedham church the
focus of his design. The simple exterior of the Essex village
churches, often shadowed by clusters of trees, can give the
passer-by little notion of the charm concealed within or of the
extent of local (and sometimes more than local) history to be
gleaned therefrom. But let us consider a few exteriors first.
Some of the best of the village churches are, as I suggested,
brick-built; and if the reader thinks that brick cannot, like
stone, lend itself to ornamental relief, I suggest he takes a look
at Netteswell (Net's'll to all sons of Essex), where the brickwork
on the outside wall of the church exhibits some really delightful
relief – lions rampant, a serpent, a rabbit, roses, leaves, and
other flowers; or he might take a look at the churches of Sandon
and Layer Marney, on both of which there is some fine diapered
brickwork. At Chignal Smealey (where, incidentally, Morant,
the county's erudite historian, was one-time rector) the church
is built entirely of Tudor brick, even to the font; whilst the
really handsome towers of Sandon and Fryerning churches and

the porch and nave of Feering church will surprise anybody who holds the prejudiced view that only stone gives itself to really lovely interpretation in building. And what of those, the majority of Essex churches, that are built of flint, with brick or stone for strengthening and support? I know that flint, especially the flint of Essex, which is almost entirely lacking in the ambitious flush-work of the flint of Suffolk and Norfolk, is often looked askance at, and I confess I once shared this antipathy myself; but increasing familiarity over the years has quite changed my opinion and now I wonder why I ever felt repelled by its rough, many-coloured surface, untutored as homespun cloth, changeable as the weather. I find the flint churches of Essex not only one of its loveliest features but also one of its most typical, being wholly compatible with the Essex scene and even with the Essex character. It would be futile to pick out any churches as especially to be sought for; they are to be found, in their varying appeal, all over the county; and if sometimes it is one feature that appeals, sometimes another, there is really little to choose between any of them for final fitness and desirability.

But a special word must be said of the round flint towers of the Essex churches, of which there are several, notably those at Pentlow, Lammarsh, Bardfield Saling, and Great Leigh (part of whose fabric dates back to A.D. 970). No doubt the original reason for the building of these round church towers, which are perhaps more quaint than intrinsically beautiful, was to avoid the expense of securing brick or stone for strengthening at the corners. They were an architectural device, in fact, and not, as might be supposed, a local whimsey. But at Pentlow a more curious explanation is given. "Before the Flood" (I quote from an old number of *Notes and Queries*) "it had been used as a well, and when the inhabitants of the new generations, who resided on that spot, were looking for a place to build a church, they selected this site because the old well would do for a steeple, and therefore they built the church to it, as it now stands."

For many people, however, the really characteristic church architecture of Essex is neither flint nor stone nor brick nor a blend of either of these: it is wood. And there is this, if no more, to be said for their choice, that Essex was pre-eminently the forest county. (Incidentally, in a county that contains part of the cornbelt and is therefore very straw-conscious, it is strange, and I think a pity, that there are no examples of thatched churches in Essex.) There is a special charm about the little wooden churches, tucked away among the trees. Blackmore, Thundersley, West Hanningford, and Mountnessing are all good examples. The narrowly tapering belfries, whose shingles shine a silver-grey, fit most harmoniously into the scene; and when to these are added the finely worked porches (of which the one at South Benfleet is surely without equal, not only in the county but in the whole land) the effect is altogether delightful. But of course the best-known example of a wooden Essex church is the one at Greenstead, near Ongar, where the nave is entirely constructed of the trunks of big oak-trees, split, roughly hewed on both sides, and fastened in place with huge wooden pins. It is to be doubted whether, as is popularly supposed, this is the basis of the actual wooden chapel which was erected to shelter the body of St Edmund when, on its journey from London to Bury, it rested here. The more likely supposition is that some sort of rough shelter was built on this spot and that the church was erected afterwards to commemorate the event. However this may have been, it seems certain that the place was somehow associated with St Edmund and that the church is one of the oldest we have in the county. Another curious Essex church, by the way, is that of Little Maplestead. It is one of the four ancient round churches in England and the smallest of them all. Originally it was a church of the Knights Hospitallers of St John of Jerusalem, who had a preceptory here, as they did at Temple Cressing.

We know too little of the designers and builders of England's village churches. For this reason alone, it always gives me a sense of satisfaction to find them even named. Essex, fortunately, has remembered several of its church builders and honoured them (they were usually Tudor men) with appropriate tablets. In the wall of the fine old brick tower of Castle Hedingham church, for instance, there is set a memorial tablet proudly announcing the fact that Robert Archer was "the master builder of this stepell, 1616." Toppesfield similarly commemorates the builder of "ye steple, anno 1699" – also the churchwarden at the time; whilst Anthony Gould, who built the tower of Terling church, is also named.

But what of the treasures housed inside these Essex village churches? In what way, you may ask, do they merit the claim I have made that they are especially worthy of the attention of the curious? I do not pretend to know every village church in Essex, though I know a good many; and it may well be that there is much in them for me yet to discover; but it seems to me that the best I can do here is to enumerate some of the things I have seen and which have particularly appealed to me. I remember, for example, puzzling a long time over an inscription I had copied from a framed piece of wood hanging on the wall inside the little church of Ashen. It read thus:

THIS HATH BIN THE CHURCH
ING THE MEARRING STOOLE
AND SO IT SHALL BE STILL
1620.

It was by the good offices of Mr G. Eland that I finally solved this little riddle. The piece of wood was the seat of a stool or chair intended to be used for the marriage service and for the churching of women. There were of course very few seats for general use in our churches in early times (and such a tiny church as Ashen may well have had none at all) and so it seems natural that such seats as there were should have been ear-marked for their special purpose.

Then, at one time and another, I have collected a number of epitaphs from various Essex churches, of which the following are among the more interesting:

Shee on this clayen pillow laid her head,
As Brides doe use, the first to go to bed.
He mist her soon, and yet ten months he trys
To live apart, but liks it not, and dys.

(Margaretting.)

She was – but room denies to tell the what.
Summe all perfections uppe: and she was that.

(Abbots Roding.)

Learne so to live by Faythe, as I have lived before.
Learne so to give by Faythe, as I did at my Doore.
Learne so to keep by Faythe, as God he still thy store.
Learne so to lend by Faythe, as I did to the Poore.
Learne so to live to give to keep to lend and spend

That God in trust at day of death may prove thy friend.
>   (Stebbing: Isaac Bernard, Yeoman.)

> Rare was the roote, the branches bravely spred,
> And some still are, though some be withered,
> Two of the precious ones (a piteous spoile)
> Were ill transplanted to a foreign soile,
> Where the hot sunne (how ere it did befall)
> Drew up their juice, to perfume heaven withall.
> When will the heaven such flowers to th'earth repay
> As th'earth afforded heaven, two in a day.

>   (Little Easton.)

At Birdbrook a tombstone commemorates the death of one
Martha Blewitt of the Swan Inn at Baythorn End, who was the
wife of nine husbands in succession. The text of her funeral
sermon, so the tombstone tells us, was: "Last of all the woman
died also." And finally, at Great Canfield, when the tomb of
Francis Penwerne (died 1722) was for some reason taken up
about forty years later, there was discovered on the back of it an
epitaph for one of the Wiseman family. What queer frugality, I
wonder, could this have concealed?

Mural paintings in churches have always fascinated me, as
much for their primitive art as for the hint they give of the days
when all the walls and pillars and ceilings and tombs and
chantries were so gaily decorated that the whole building must
have blazed with colour. Sometimes these murals were merely
decorative patterns, but sometimes they were pictorial representations of holy stories. In the latter case they were, in fact,
the illiterate peasants' bible, where he might read in pictures
those biblical stories which he could not read in words. The
picture of St Christopher was always a favourite. Its usual place
was on the north wall, by the door, where all might see him as
they trooped out of church and asked his protection in their
everyday comings and goings. In Essex there are some excellent
St Christophers, among the best examples being those at Little
Baddow, Layer Marney, Canewdon, Feering, Ingatestone,
Latton, Fairstead, and Ongar. Of these the first two are the
best, the Little Baddow St Christopher, with his smiling,
bearded face, being especially fine in draughtsmanship and
attractive in colour. The Layer Marney St Christopher occurs,

most unusually, at the east end of the nave and was somewhat touched up in the 'eighties. Nevertheless, it is very fine. It is large, clear, and has some good reds and greens in it. I like especially the stylised waves washing round the saint's feet (one of which seems to have an eel twisted up the ankle) and the old man's big-featured, honest-to-goodness face. He would inspire confidence in any hesitant traveller. Touching up has been the ruin of too many mural paintings, for which reason I often prefer the brief fragments to such total recoveries as, for instance, the paintings at Copford. At Copford, however, there is, in addition to the repainted and touched up vaulting of the apse, an altogether unusual figure composition, untouched and in fairly good condition, depicting the healing of Jairus's daughter. Professor Tristram, the greatest authority on English church murals, goes so far as to say of this painting that "the fairness and beauty of its colour, together with the expressive and sensitive rendering of the subject, entitles it to rank among the finest examples of English workmanship." (Incidentally, it was Professor Tristram who superintended the uncovering of the mural fragments at Fairstead church, of which the Last Supper, including a sinister figure representing Judas, and the journey into Jerusalem are the most arresting.) In any case, nobody should miss this little church at Copford, not far from Colchester, if only for its lovely setting among the bushy meadows and its deep sense of rural peace. A sixpenny pamphlet is provided for the convenience of visitors and it is a model of what such things should be: brief and factual. Our village churches everywhere are the local history books, but they need interpreting to the stranger. A short guidebook, such as Copford provides, not only does a service to the general public but could be made remunerative to the church; and it might well be part of the vicar's duty, if not his pleasure, to see that his church is thus served. Substantiated facts are all the visitor requires: the moralisings and exhortations so often accompanying church guidebooks are an unwelcome intrusion upon his enjoyment.

Screens, such as are the pride of Devonshire churches, are few and far between in Essex. Moreover, even where they still exist, they have often been cut down to the level of the pews. The most outstanding screen in the county is the one at Great Bardfield, which, extraordinarily enough, is of stone. It is beautifully wrought. For the rest, there are minimised screens at

Rickling, Wimbish, Castle Hedingham, and Stambourne, this last one being painted in each panel with figures of unidentifiable saints or kings. Early stained windows, too, are rare, the county having suffered its share of damage from war and the zeal of the Puritans. A remarkably fine specimen of a Stem-of-Jesse window (fourteenth century) survives, however, at Margaretting. To the destruction and vandalism of yesterday has now to be added the further destruction by bombing in the last war. Essex was directly in the line of attack on London and was itself a favourite target because of its many airfields. One of the greatest losses was through the bombing of the great "wool" church of Coggeshall, where the fine embattled tower and the spacious nave were entirely ruined. Danbury too suffered similarly, though some of the famous (crusaders' tombs in the church remain intact. And Black Notley church, where the great Essex naturalist John Ray was buried, was badly damaged; but both church and tomb have now been restored.

Finally, a word about church barrel-organs and ringers' jars. I remember Dr Percy Scholes once telling me (and he of all people should know) that Essex exceeded all other counties in the number of barrel-organs late in use in its churches; and indeed I believe the barrel-organ in Barnston church, just outside Dunmow, is still used to accompany the hymns. But I confess ringers' jars appeal to me more than barrel-organs. These curiosities were almost entirely confined to the eastern counties and were specially favoured in Essex. Surviving examples are still to be seen in Bocking and Colchester and (just over the border) Clare. They held from three to four gallons; had two handles; were decorated and fitted at the base with a hole for a spigot. But let me quote Mr Alfred Hills, of Braintree, an authority on all antiquarian aspects of Essex life and customs. "One New Year's Eve," he says, "this imposing piece was carried round the town from house to house, to receive a mixture of beer, wine, and spirits known as 'hot pot.' It was then stood on a block in the centre of the belfry and drawn from as occasion might require. ..." Certainly they were stout ringers in those days.

Not being an emphatic admirer of ruined Norman castles, I cannot feel unduly perturbed that Essex is so poorly supplied with these. Certainly there is no other county, as Dr P. H.

Reaney has declared, that "bears so strongly as Essex the imprint of the Norman Conquest"; but happily, at least so far as I am concerned, it is an imprint that is to be found in place-names rather than in grim stone relics. I like to know that the lordly Alex de la Peri is still remembered, all these hundreds of years later, in Perry Meadow; or that Twitty Fee (what a genius Essex has for the incongruous name!) commemorates one William Twitye, who came over with the Conqueror; or that Cuckoo Farm, far from being the special haunt of that amoral bird, merely intends us to know that its original fourteenth-century owner was Walter Cukkook. These airy fancies (and no fancies either) are for me a much better memorial to our Norman lords and masters than the tumbled stones of their bold, assertive castles. I make no excuse therefore for relegating Essex castles to a brief epilogue: their fewness, if not their general unattractiveness, would alone warrant such a treatment.

Chief of such castle remains today in Essex are those of Colchester and Castle Hedingham. No doubt for those who have a mind for sermons in stones the former is eloquent enough. It is built mainly of Roman brick, taken most likely from the many Roman ruins in the city; and its keep is by far the largest of all the Norman keeps in this country. For the rest, it houses a fine museum where the visitor may ponder at leisure over all that remains today of the ancient settlement of Camulodunum. (He will probably prefer to spend his time among the interesting collection of Essex bygones, where he may learn how the world went about its business somewhat nearer his own time.) Fine as Colchester castle is, however, Hedingham castle surely bears the palm for the imposing nature of its position in the surrounding landscape. Approaching the town, beside the narrow Colne, the castle keep is seen rising four-square above the clustering trees, a landmark for many miles around. The castle was built between 1088 and 1107 by Aubrey de Vere. Its rubble walls, up to twelve feet thick, are encased in squared Barnack stone, and the whole terrifying keep (all that today remains of the castle) provides the visitor, on those very rare occasions when he is allowed to see over it, with a fairly clear and anyhow sufficient reminder of the kind of life that was led by the nobles and their rough soldiery in those turbulent times. He may see in what little, slit-like rooms, cut in the walls, the lord and his family had their sleeping quarters, and he may even, if he is so disposed, probe the intimacies of Norman sanitation.

Of Pleshey castle nothing remains today but a single- span brick bridge crossing the deep fosse to the mount where stood for four hundred years the home of the High Constable of England. If there is nothing to see in the way of ruins, I certainly do not complain: rather, I find it a most pleasant place, especially in spring, when the nightingale sings in the thickets of the fosse and the scent of the hawthorn blossom lingers over the hummocky mount. It is an ideal place for a picnic – and what better purpose would it have served, if its ruins still survived, tidied up and docketed and narrowly tended by the Office of Works? Other Essex castles include those of Saffron Walden, Stansted Mountfitchet, Ongar, Clavering, Stebbing, Rayleigh, Hadleigh (immortalised in Turner's sombre picture), Steeple Bumpstead and Mount Bures. These have little to show but heaps of fallen masonry; and I cheerfully commit them all to the loving care of the indefatigable antiquarian.

CHAPTER III

Round and About the Villages and Towns

ESSEX is the walker's countryside. It is true that his journey will be the more fruitful if he knows enough about agriculture to understand something of what is going on in the fields and farms; but even without this advantage he will find ample reward in passing through village after village of great charm and intense individuality. A good centre to start from would be Newport, which is fairly easily accessible on the main London-to-Cambridge road or railway and from which he can conveniently explore that strange hinterland of the chalk ridge, from Elmdon to the two Chishalls, and round home again by Clavering and Quendon. Here is the county's outpost – a region unlike any other in the way it farms (and therefore, to some extent, in the way it lives) and yet unmistakably Essex and full of interest.

Newport itself is worth the closest attention. For several years I passed daily down the long, single street on which the village is based and never once lost the thrill of its so various houses and cottages. For part of the way these are set high above the road on a grass-verged causeway – a feature of the village, as it is of some other villages in this north-west corner of the county. Where the road (and railway) cross the diminutive Cam there is, for instance, a plaster and timber-framed house which takes its name from the crown over its fine, shell-shaped porch. Crown House, they say, was occupied by Nell Gwyn, as being conveniently on the way, presumably, to her adoring monarch at Newmarket. The evidence for this bit of local history, however, does not seem to be very circumstantial, since the date over the house is 1692 (the year in which it was built?) and Nell Gwyn died in 1687. Nearby are the remains of a priory. All down the street, in fact, are a quite exceptional assortment of old houses, ranging from Tudor to Georgian; but perhaps the one which will detain the visitor longest is the so-called Monks

Barn. The timbers here are filled with an attractive brick-nogging; and there is an oriel window supported on a carved base whereon is a representation of the Coronation of the Virgin Mary, with on one side an angel harpist, and on the other an angel playing upon a pair of organs.

On the grass verge at the Shortgrove end of the village is a curious old stone – a weathered slab of reddish-brown sandstone. It is called the Lepers' Stone and is supposed to have been the stone in whose cavity coins were laid as an offering in return for food placed there by Brethren of the Lepers' Hospital close by. Perhaps in still earlier times the stone was a local meeting-place where (according to W. Giles) "obligations were sanctified by the usual pagan invocation to their gods, with offerings of food and libations which afterwards became the portion of the poor"; in which case its associations with charity are very old indeed, and this Newport Lepers' Stone, which hundreds of people pass every day in their cars as they speed towards London, is one of the most to-be-treasured relics in the county. It is said that the stone, which is now considerably buried, was blown down in a great storm towards the close of the eighteenth century, to the consternation of the inhabitants, who regarded the event as an omen of disaster – a proof of the regard with which the stone was held in the common memory. Glasshouses for the growing of carnations now stand on the site of the Lepers' Hospital, but portions of the pillars of its chapel have been built into the brick wall of Shortgrove Park. Further still along this same road is a turning leading to Saffron Walden and known as Gallows Hill – doubtless the same gallows mentioned in the Walden records of 1597 ("The carpenter for setting up the gallows, 3/- [three shillings]"; and again: "Payed to Stanmer for 2 halters, 4*d*." [four old pence]) and of 1631 ("Payed for tymber for making gallows, 4/4 [four shillings and fourpence]").

But for me at least the final appeal of Newport rests on neither its houses nor its Lepers' Stone nor its church (celebrated for its painted thirteenth-century chest, one of the few examples in England of early painting on wood, the Virgin and three Saints being portrayed on the lid), but rather on London Lane and the Meads. London Lane is a green and overgrown cart-track which ran from Newport to Rickling: it possibly went further, but I never traced it. Originally it was a recognised road along which wagonloads of hay and corn were taken, bells jingling, to London. And now, writing of those forgotten hayloads, I am reminded of a passage in Reginald A. Beckett's *Romantic Essex,* one of the very best books, despite its title, on the county, full of sensitive appreciation and original observation. Beckett is writing (in 1900) of the country outside Brentwood, but he might just as well have been writing of London Lane as I heard old men tell of it. "Here at night the only sign of life beyond the lights in the inn parlours is the string of haycarts on their way to London for the early market. The fragrant load is piled well forward over the shafts and balanced by a corresponding weight overhanging behind; the horses steam in the light of the lanterns as they plod along the road, guided mainly by their own intelligence, while the weary carter, who may have been at work since daybreak, is perhaps unconsciously qualifying for an appearance before the magistrates on a charge of 'riding asleep'." Such grassy cart-tracks and lanes, now mainly overgrown, are common enough in Essex and a very real part of its charm; but London Lane, with its brilliant spindle-berries in autumn and its cowslips in spring, always seems to me to have more charm than most. The Meads, when I knew them well, consisted of a great stretch of wasteland, part common, part marsh, stretching east from the village towards Debden Park. A farmer might hire some of the Meads for a bit of rough grazing; but otherwise they had no use – and that was their very appeal. They had become thereby the haunt of all manner of unusual birds, wild animals, and flowers. Marsh orchises abounded among the tussocks of reed grass, rare fungi and snakes; and I even heard of a hoopoe being seen there in or about 1917. Now, unhappily, the Meads, like most other such one-time wastes, have been called upon to add their mite to our quota of food production, and part of the place is a (no doubt necessary) sewage farm.

Of the several attractive villages west of Newport I would draw attention in particular to Arkesden, sheltered among its trees, a shady village of thatched cottages and flowery gardens and a strong, lively individuality in its inhabitants. Further in lies Clavering, of whose castle nothing remains today but a tree-filled moat, and whose church, lighted with fine clerestory windows, dwarfs the swallow-haunted row of old cottages (perhaps they were once almshouses) at its gate. Not far away is

Berden, on the border of Hertfordshire, where a boy bishop is still crowned each December in St Nicholas's church. "Scholars on St Nicholas's Day" (so Brand tells us in his *Observations on Popular Antiquities*) "elected three out of their number, one of whom was to play the Bishop, the other two the parts of deacons. The Bishop was escorted by his fellows in solemn procession to church, where, with his mitre on, he presided during the time of divine worship. At its conclusion he and his deacons went about singing from door to door, and collected money, not begging it as alms, but demanding it as the Bishop's subsidy."

As one climbs to the chalk ridge the villages become more isolated and the countryside in general has an air of remoteness: here, one feels, the life of the fields is all. It is a region of almost continuous ploughland – few roads, but many foot-paths and cart-tracks; few houses. The crop yields, too, if excellent in quality are small in quantity. Passing through such scattered hamlets as Duddenhoe End, for instance, one has the impression that life must always have been near the bone here, at least for the labourers who lived in these little thatched cottages. The settlements get closer and more populous as one descends from the chalk. Even Wendens Ambo, with its diminutive, Saxon-towered church and its mighty oak barn on the farm close by, seems by comparison alert and anyway companionable, as also does Littlebury, further north along the main road, where in the seventeenth century lived the whimsical Mr Winstanley, famous for the practical jokes he played on his guests. Says Defoe, of this gentleman: "He had made many odd Contrivances of Chairs running on Springs, etc., which usually much surprised Strangers who came to see the House. The Person appointed to shew it generally placed the greatest Stranger into a particular Chair, which, on touching the Spring, ran backward through the House into the Garden." Winstanley also designed a "Water Theatre," I suppose rather after the fashion on the Continent at this time, "full of ingenious contrivances," which long amused the habitués of Piccadilly; and for seven years he laboured to construct a lighthouse on the Eddystone Rock, where both he and it were finally swept away on a winter's night of great storm.

Saffron Walden must be reckoned as one of the most delightful towns to explore in all East Anglia. The best view of it is from the Cross at the top of High Street: the wide, tree-bordered street dips to the centre of the town, and dominating all stands the great church with its fine Late Perpendicular spire. Narrow streets branch off at right angles and there is not one that lacks some house of unusual appeal. Most famous of all, of course, is the so-called Sun Inn, in Church Street, parts of which date back to the fourteenth century, and which is said to have been Cromwell's headquarters in 1646. On the plaster of the over-hanging front are some of the most astonishing examples of pargework in the whole country, its subject-matter ranging from birds and flowers that have no like on this earth to similarly unnatural men, with club, sword and buckler – and even stray human feet. But if the Sun Inn is the most spectacular of Walden's early houses, there are others of no less, though quieter, appeal, especially perhaps on the Audley End side of the town. Then there is an antique maze, consisting of a number of concentric circles surrounded by an embankment – a toy of unknown origin unless it be, as some suppose, an ancient local meeting-place such as we have already noted in Newport, in which case it is almost certainly the oldest one known to exist.

Through the yard of the Rose and Crown, where the farmers gather on market-day, one passes to the wide Common, a play-ground of some fifteen acres, never so lively as on the Saturday before mid-Lent, when it is given over to swings and round-abouts and all the other gaudy paraphernalia of a fair. A very different sort of celebration took place here on July 6, 1814, "to enable the poor to partake of the general joy of their country and of Europe, upon the glorious occasion of the return of peace." A revealing description of the occasion was made by one William Robinson, surveyor to the town, from which we learn that, at a meeting held to arrange the details for the celebra-tion, "it was resolved that Mr John Player do provide an ox," that Messrs Spicer, Adams and Gatward jointly provide another ox, "all of the very best quality ... at 11s. 8d. [eleven shillings and eightpence] per stone, and also that they provide about 7 stone of suet each." The Common was chosen as being the most suitable place because "it has a fine turf upon chalk which soon becomes dry and pleasant to the promenader." So the poor of Saffron Walden were bidden to the feast, "each person and family to come neatly dressed, and to bring small mugs or glasses, knives, forks, etc., for their own use, and to take their plates, knives and forks into their baskets as soon as dinner is over and send them home." It seems that Saffron Walden was always very proper in its manners, and what a world of fore-thought there was in that "small mugs." Silence was to be observed on the sound of a bugle, when grace would be said at every table both before and after meat. "Industrious mechanics" were to serve as "waiters and tapsters," whilst the "yeomen and gentry, by their kind and Christian condescension" would carve the joints. After which there were to be donkey races, jumping in sacks, jingling (whatever sort of frolic this may have been), foot races, and, to end up with, fireworks. Altogether it required seventy-five tables "all in a vast oval" to seat the 2,600 persons who were invited, and the charge on the town was £310 12*s*. 11*d*. Here was "strength through joy" indeed! Is it being too improbable, I wonder, to see in this amusing mixture of gener-osity and strict decorum the hand of the Quakers? Anyway, I think their descendants in the town today would be the first to smile and say it might have been so. The Society of Friends became established in Saffron Walden as early as 1639 and the town is still coloured by their beneficent influence. A spacious Friends School is indeed one of its features. I suspect that the Quakers were also largely responsible for the fact that the London-to-Cambridge railway was not allowed to run through the town, so that to-day a small branch line connects with Audley End. If such a veto occasioned a certain amount of inconvenience, it probably also had the compensating effect of helping to preserve the place's calm and unruffled aspect.

Generally speaking I have no great fondness for provincial museums. A bird on the wing communicating its joy in life to the observer, though so fleetingly seen, is infinitely more valu-able to us than a bird in a glass case communicating its sadness in a dusty death. Besides, the exhibits are often so heaped about the place that, even if we can find them, they are devoid of character; and sometimes the best exhibits are not exhibited at all. I remember one day visiting the Colchester Museum, whose various collections are admittedly very fine indeed. On this occasion I wanted to see the early Essex implements and bygones, only to be told that they were shut away in the cellars. "The job of a museum," I was informed, "is to collect and not to exhibit." For the most part, therefore, I avoid country museums. But of the Saffron Walden Museum I gladly make an exception and even go so far as to recommend it to all visitors to the town. Its collection of Essex antiquities is a most instructive one; and it would have been even more so if the treasures which were unearthed in the Bartlow Hills, between 1832 and 1840, had not been privately housed in Easton Lodge, where they were nearly all lost in a fire. The Bartlow Hills consist of a group of six tumuli which seem to have marked the site of the burial place of a wealthy and important family, either of Roman colonists or, more possibly, of Romanised descendants of British tribal princes. Sacrificial ewers of bronze, beautifully ornamented, grave furniture, lamps, bottles of earthenware were among the relics brought to light.

Not far from the Bartlow Hills is the village of Ashdon, gateway to that wide stretch of country by the Cambridgeshire border where the undulating fields of chalkland, with their infrequent farmsteads hidden among sheltering trees, provide an altogether new landscape and one that is especially lovely in August, when, so far as the eye can see, there is little but the ripening gold of corn. For me the particular attraction of Ashdon is its old post windmill. One climbs the wide flight of steps and enters by the double hatch from which, in former days, the miller could take his view over the surrounding countryside, lord indeed of all he surveyed. But there is no miller now to lean over the hatch and watch the wagons come rumbling up the lane with corn to be ground. The mill is no longer in use; and, as one rambles through it, one gets the almost uncanny impression that work stopped here as dramatically as it did on that fatal day in Pompeii: the miller's tools and tackle still lie about (or did, when I was there a couple of harvests ago) as if he had but left them for the moment and would pick them up again by and by. Incidentally, among them was an eighteenth-century steel-yard with painted scrollwork; and there were other pieces of wrought-iron work that seemed to betray the same craftsmanship. The date of the mill, 1763, was scratched on one of the beams. Best of all, perhaps, was to climb the ladders to the top floor and stand under the curving, weather-boarded roof that is like a white boat turned upside down. Through the little square windows, lightless now, one gazed over one of the most productive stretches of corn country anywhere. There, all before one, were the blue-shadowed stooks in the yellow stubble-field; but the mill that should have ground them into flour was idle and falling to pieces. A little way out of the village stands the church, its stone-embattled tower all but hidden among trees. I liked the way the cottages opened on to the churchyard, so that the inhabitants of one of them had made a flower-garden on either side of the path that ran between the tombs.

As good as Newport, for a walker's centre, is Thaxted, save that it is somewhat more difficult to get at. An antiquated branch railway from Elsenham, on the main line, brings the visitor; and even then it sets him down a good mile out of the town. Or there is a daily 'bus service to and from London. Anyway, once the visitor has arrived, there awaits his discovery the very best of Essex and all within an easy radius of the town. "Is this really Essex?" asks the prejudiced stranger, imbued with the usual notion that the whole county is flat and dull. "All these views? All these ups-and-downs? All these lovely old cottages and sunny cornfields?" Yes, indeed: this is Essex, the best of it, the heart of it. Here you can listen to a speech that has hardly changed through the centuries. Here you can find villagers who still do the good old-fashioned things for the good old-fashioned reasons – threshing their seed beans with the flail, trimming their cottage hedges to the shapes of crowns and birds and who-knows-what, wearing their caps on their knees when they go a-visiting, and planting their potatoes at the foot of the Cross on Good Friday. Here, in fact, you can find that Essex which, though at some considerable expense in the matter of progress, keeps still the essential character we inevitably associate with this and only this county. Almost any one of the villages within easy distance of Thaxted – the Hedinghams, the Belchamps, the 'fields – offers an irresistible appeal. And if, in writing here about these particular villages, I omit any one attraction in favour of another, it is because my space and certainly not my liking is limited.

Of Thaxted itself I have already written, for in a sense Thaxted *is* its church. The great spire of it dominates the place, the religion (and politics) of it colour the life of the community, and one way or another it draws to the little town a considerable number of visitors. There may be no roaring furnaces in Thaxted today, no clacking looms; the wool merchants do not offer their wares in the market place, the Guild of Cutlers does not come teeming into the church, with hymn and banner, to supplicate its patron saint, Lawrence, whose emblem still hangs in the chancel; but the men and women of this diminished place are close-bound, now as then, to the great church that juts against their daily skies. However, here are other attractions which the visitor will quickly discover. Overlooking the main street is a timber-framed, overhung Cutlers Guild Hall of great age and much beauty. Its open ground floor was once used as a market hall; but now its main use would seem to be as a convenient prop and stay for the old men of the town, where they may loll out of the rain and watch the world go by. Thaxted still has its charter, granted away back in Queen Mary's reign; but it seems somehow characteristic of the town that some time afterwards the mayor and corporation meekly surrendered their offices and have since never been succeeded. Then again, close by the Guild Hall there is a quite astonishing example of a timber-framed Tudor house, overhanging the cobbled lane that leads sharply up to the church. What its authentic earliest history may be I do not know, but it is supposed at some time to have been Dick Turpin's house. Thaxted, in fact, is full of such rewarding architecture, from the converted row of single storey alms-houses beside the churchyard to the vicarage with its enormous yew hedge, and from the fine brick Georgian house immediately opposite the church to the bow-windowed Victorian shops in the High Street. Seemingly certain sections of the town still like to imagine they are living in the medieval merry England which some of their architecture suggests, for on festival days one may hear the scrape of fiddles and see the Morris dancers come treading their antique measure down the street.

West of Thaxted lie the 'fields – Finchingfield, Great and Little Bardfield, Toppesfield, Wethersfield, and Gosfield, than which I swear there is no lovelier group of villages in all the county. These are in some of the best farming country and it is hardly an exaggeration to say that their whole outlook is conditioned by the seasonal husbandry. Even if all the cottagers do not these days work in the fields, at least they have not yet lost their interest and intimate concern for what goes on there. Ride on one of the 'buses that connect these communities with the neighbouring towns and you may find yourself surprised at the specialised interest shown in the work of the fields through which it passes. This is true even when the 'bus is mostly filled with women; for it is ingrained in the women of these villages that for part at least of the year they will work in the fields – an occupation which, for its companionableness, its healthiness, and the relief it offers from the daily domestic routine, they would not miss and at which they sometimes earn very high money. Or go into the tap-room of one of the village pubs here and you will find that nine-tenths of the conversation concerns itself with agriculture or its allied activities, and especially is this so in summer, as the days draw nearer to harvest and the men arrive for their evening glass of beer with outsize ears of corn in their button-holes.

Many amenities have come to these villages in recent years: electric light, if not yet to all of them, regular and frequent 'bus services into the towns, new council cottages, complete with bathroom and the officially recognised cubic feet of air space (not to mention a hundred and one restrictions), and even, in some cases, a visiting once-a-week cinema; but they still remain as intensely rural as if they were two hundred instead of half a hundred miles from London. In one thing, however, the 'fields are changing rapidly. Each of them is a parish of unusually large acreage, with, in addition to the village community itself, many remote and outlying groups of cottages, called variously Ends or Greens or Streets. More and more these strongholds of rural individuality and idiosyncracy are being forsaken for the more populous centres. The men may still prefer the isolation inherent in these hamlets and outlying groups (and not only for their nearness to the farm where they work), but the women increasingly dislike it: for the sake of the education of their children, as well as for their own convenience, they insist on moving into the villages, to be at the focus of such life as there is, near the shops and the 'buses, nearer the towns. To some extent, therefore, the 'fields are gradually losing something of their character, for it was especially in these outlying "uplands" that they retained their strongest hold on the manners and customs and speech of days gone by.

Of all the 'fields, Great Bardfield had, until recent years, pre-eminence, for it was once a small market town, complete with market cross, and a centre of the spinning industry. Even until comparatively lately its annual fair was a source of considerable attraction to the district, especially for its ponies and horses tethered in the street and for its evening merry-makings. Old men in the locality still date their garden husbandry by this fair. Dwindled though Great Bardfield is today, it nevertheless

retains a distinct character of its own and, chiefly by the aid of
the several artists who have made it their home in recent years,
even contributes not inconsiderably to the greater world
outside. It is a village of the single-street pattern, wide and
well-planned, and attractive for the variety of periods its architecture spans. In one of its houses lived Queen Elizabeth's
Serjeant-at-Arms: the Bendlowes monogram may be seen on the
corner-post. Elizabeth herself when a young princess is said to
have been kept here in hiding from Mary. Its history of yesterday, however, is by no means its only charm today: behind its
pleasant façade it hides one of the loveliest gardens I know. The
rooks caw in the trees down by its stream – the village church
framed in their boughs – and every season brings new joys to
light, from the golden pollen dropping from the old cedar in
summer to the snowdrops whitening the ground beneath the
hazel wood in spring. Some way outside the village is another
old house of fame, though now it is falling to pieces and unoccupied. In Great Lodge lived the famous Lumley family, of whom
Sir Martin was the Lord Mayor of London in 1620 and several of
whose later members were sheriffs of the county. The mile-long
walk whereby the family came to church is now only a cart-
track, though some of its pollarded elms still stand. Little
Bardfield is, if anything, too picturesque, several of its thatched
cottages having been extensively reconditioned and rather coyly
decorated in a style that certainly has little to do with the "folk."
Its Hall, with the old church hidden in its grounds, is modern
and nothing to dwell upon, though it is pleasantly situated
among some fine trees and claims the attention of the passer-by
with a Jacobean leaden figure (of a man shooting) that can be
seen from the road.

But if Great Bardfield had precedence in the matter of
importance, Finchingfield must surely always have had precedence in the matter of sheer attractiveness. Journalists, whose
irresponsible labels are apt to stick, have delighted to call
Finchingfield one of the four or five loveliest villages in
England: this time they may even be right. Certainly it is of the
kind that immediately brings an exclamation of pleasure from
strangers when they first come upon its many-charactered
houses spread around the spacious Green. It is this Green,
crossed by four converging roads and split by a brook, that gives
the village much of its individuality. Swallows skim, blue-

backed, over the water, which now passes under a narrow brick bridge but which once was crossed by a ford – as gypsies, steadfast to old habits, still prove on occasion and get stuck fast in the mud in consequence. Greens were provided by our forefathers for pleasure as well as use, and Finchingfield Green never looks better than on the evening of some day of celebration, when the edges of its several segments are looped with flag-streamers and hung with fairy-lights. There is even a Continental look about the place at all times, as of some hill village in the south of France, where the jumbled roofs climb to the crowning, all-dominating church. An additional attraction to the lay-out of the village is its high Causeway, which lifts the footpath passengers level with the tops of the loads of corn and straw passing through the streets. One of these is called Duck End and contains an old post windmill, her diminished sails set at St Andrew's Cross, as they should be when a mill is at rest; and it is perhaps typical of the conscious sense of responsibility in the villagers for the treasures they have inherited that recently they bought the mill by public subscription, to preserve her for posterity.

It would take me far beyond the bounds of this book if I attempted to do justice to this entrancing old village; but something must be said of its singular claim to have possessed a squire who kept silence for seven years. This seventeenth-century squire was William Kempe, of Spain's Hall, who, for certain words which he let fall to the dishonour of his wife, made the astonishing vow that he would keep silence for seven years – and did so. Personally, I should think a purposely silent husband must have been more of a strain to the good lady than any amount of abuse; and indeed, so she seems to have found it, for she died before his vow was completed. In any case, William Kempe achieved both for himself and for the village over which he presided something approaching notoriety. A further oddity of the man was that he chose to beguile the silent time by digging ponds, the traces of some of which may be seen in the copse behind the Hall. A memorial tablet in the church commemorates Kempe's strange penance and informs us that he was "Pious, Just, Hospitable, Master of himselfe soe much, that what others scarce doe by force and penalties, Hee did by a Voluntary constancy, Hold his peace Seaven Yeares, who was interred June ye 10, 1628, Aged 73."

It should be added, perhaps, that the name of the village has nothing to do with the quantities of finches that frequent its fields. Place-names, it is as well to remember, are a trap for the unwary. "Field" in this case does not mean a field at all in our present-day sense; it comes, in fact, from the Old English "feld" meaning quite the opposite, a stretch of unenclosed land. For the Forest of Essex stopped short at Stane Street and so the Hundred of Hinckford, in which lie all the 'fields, was never afforested and the parishes were, in contrast to the rest of Essex, worked on the open-field system. Finchingfield was therefore a settlement of long occupation. And "Finch"? One of the early ways of spelling Finchingfield was Phincingfelda, and it is most likely that "Phincing" derives from the name of its original lord and owner.

Anyone passing through the long, single street of the nearby village of Stambourne will be sure to notice its extraordinary display of clipped yew-trees of great age – especially in one garden where they do indeed "crowd into a shade." What he may not notice is a long yew hedge running at right angles to the road in the garden of the Manse. It is a hedge with certain associations; and if it is rather spoiled at the moment by having been severely cut back, perhaps time will restore it to some of its former beauty. The pastor of Stambourne Congregational Church in the first half of the nineteenth century was James Spurgeon, grandfather of the famous preacher of the Metropolitan Tabernacle. It was this venerable old man's habit to pace up and down the grass walk behind this yew hedge pursuing his holy meditations; and it was here that he sat his little grandson on his knee and foretold that he would one day become the foremost preacher in the land. In later years the illustrious preacher honoured the village where he used to visit as a lad by writing a book about it. At least, so you would suppose from its title: *Memories of Stambourne,* by C. H. Spurgeon. In fact, it is mostly written by other hands and Spurgeon's own part is far more concerned with matters celestial than terrestrial. However, the little book does give an idea of the low state into which such Essex villages as Stambourne had sunk in the 'sixties. Of the hundred and five cottages in the place ("which could hardly be less picturesque") one-fourth were vacant and some were in ruin "owing to the migration of the labourers during the last few years." Also: "there were few farmers resident in the parish, most of the farms being held off-hand." For the rest, there seem to have been innumerable ducks, pigs and donkeys in the village; the ponds were "as brown and stale as foul ale"; and altogether there was "a general disorderliness of fertility, and a sense of being out of the world, and having nothing particular to do." That sense of being out of the world still somewhat persists in Stambourne. Incidentally, it is of interest to recall that Spurgeon-in-the-Pulpit was a favourite subject as a Staffordshire china ornament and examples were often to be seen on Essex cottage mantelpieces. At the other end of the village, opposite an inn of great age, there is a fine flint-towered church, where a Straw Neck is invariably to be seen decorating the chancel rails at harvest festival, and where the curious will be rewarded with several interesting interior items, including some of the best heraldic glass in the county, whereon may be traced the motto of the MacWilliam family: "Espoir me comfort." It does not seem to have helped the inhabitants of Stambourne in the 'sixties, whatever it may do today.

In the keep-crowned village of Castle Hedingham, close by, one of the buildings worth more than passing note is the Bell Inn, which, like several other old inns in Essex, notably the White Hart at Brentwood, with its fine, galleried courtyard, was a recognised stopping-place for the coaches passing through on their alarming journey to London. Mr Adrian Bell has told the tale of one of these coaches, the famous Old Bury Coach, that ran daily between the Angel Inn at Bury St Edmunds and the Green Dragon at Bishopsgate Street early in the nineteenth century. It set out at nine o'clock in the morning and the speed was fifteen miles per hour. By 1843 the coach was having to compete with the railway, which now ran as far as Chelmsford. The fare, then, for the coach, was ten shillings outside and twenty shillings inside; but two years later the railway was advertising the journey for twelve shillings and sixpence inside and seven shillings outside. The Old Bury could not compete; it reduced its fare to ten shillings outside and sixteen shillings inside, but even this concession could not prevent people from travelling the new and fashionable way, and soon the coach (1847 to be precise) stopped running altogether. But what journeys they must have been! Adrian Bell tells of another coach, The Times, which George Palmer drove between Norwich and London. It passed through Braintree. Palmer was summoned for furious driving, and one witness declared that the coach had gone through Braintree at a great pace with an old woman (the only outside passenger) shouting out "Murder!" all the way.

Braintree, a large part of which lies in the parish of Bocking, is the town which serves all the 'fields and their neighbour villages, and in its present prosperous state it is a remarkable instance of the long continuance in one place of a particular industry. The town was a cloth-making centre as far back as the fourteenth century, whilst in Elizabeth's reign it benefited considerably by the influx of Flemings who established in East Anglia the manufacture of bays and says and other woollens. (Of this manufacture I shall have more to say later.) Braintree is still a cloth manufacturing town of distinction, the silks and crapes of Messrs Courtauld and of Messrs Warner being famous far afield. As for the appeal of the town to the chance visitor, there are moderately attractive nooks and corners and the various stalls in Market Square present a lively picture on market-days; but not even the most zealous inhabitant, I imagine, could claim that Braintree has an excess of charm. The town has, in fact, travelled a long and prosperous way since that Lenten morning in the year 1600 when William Kemp, a London actor, danced into it from the Chelmsford road on the fourth day of his famous Morris dance from London to Norwich. He himself left an amusing account of the affair, which he called his "nine daies wonder." After coming as far as Chelmsford, he had set out again light-heartedly enough – "my Taberer strucke up, and lightly I tript forward"; but towards Braintree he came upon "the heaviest way that ever mad Morrice-dancer trode. This foule way I could find no ease in, thicke woods being on eyther side the lane; the lane likewise being full of deep holes, sometimes I skipt up to the waste. ..." Oh, those early Essex roads! Perhaps it was these, and not the earthbound spirit of the men and women of Braintree, that explained why nobody volunteered to tread a measure with him, as often happened elsewhere, particularly at Sudbury, over the border, where "a lusty Country lasse" asked him for some bells and said she would dance a mile with him. "I lookt upon her," says Kemp, "saw mirth in her eyes, heard boldness in her words, and beheld her ready to tucke up her russet petticoate; I fitted her with bells, which she merrily taking, garnisht her thicke short legs, and with a smooth brow bad the Taberer begin. The Drum strucke; forward marcht I with my merry Mayde-marian, who shooke her fat sides and footed it merrily. ..." But let me be quite fair to the Tudor inhabitants of Braintree. On leaving them, Kemp said: "If I should deny that I was welcome at Braintree, I should slander an honest crew of kind men, among whome I far'd well, slept well, and was every way well used."

It happens, anyway, that there is evidence that the Braintree folk of those days were more than partial to actors and acting. The early records of the parish church tell of one or two instances of this partiality. Plays, in fact, were performed in the church itself – as was not unusual then. Payment to the actors in these plays is mentioned several times in the records, whilst other items include money "for letting of the play garments," "for lending the play gear," and "for a play of St Swythyn acted in the church on a Wednesday for which was gathered £6 14s. 11d."

The whole district hereabout suffered severely from the plague at one time and another – especially during the epidemic of 1665. Dr Kidder, who was rector of the nearby parish of Rayne at the time, has left a graphic account of its horrors. "No tongue can express," he writes, "the dismal calamity which that part of Essex lay under at that time. As for myself, I was in perpetual danger. I conversed daily with those who came from infected houses and it was unavoidable. The provisions sent into Braintree were left at this village near my house. Thither the Earl of Warwick sent his fat bullocks, which he did every week give to the poor of Braintree. The servants were not willing to carry them further. This occasioned frequent coming from that most infected place to my village and indeed to my very door. My parish clerk had it when he put on my surplice, and went from me to his house, and died. Another neighbour had three children, and they all died in three nights immediately succeeding each other, and I was forced to carry them all to the churchyard and bury them. We were alarmed continually with the news of death and awakened to expect our own true turns. This continued a great part of the summer. It pleased God to preserve me and all mine from the noisome pestilence. Praised be his name."

Some ten miles east of Braintree lies Coggeshall, a little town which at one time was even more famous for its cloth manufacture; but now this industry has died out altogether and the place is largely supported by its seed-growing. Both here and in the neighbouring Kelvedon the fields are small and sown with flowers for seed. One turns a corner and comes suddenly upon a field of scarlet salvias, bold as a trumpet call, or acres of fragrant sweet peas. In autumn too the careful harvest provides an unusual and interesting prospect. If Coggeshall is a great deal sleepier today than Braintree, it is also a great deal pleasanter to saunter in. It has no railway and depends for its means of communication on the 'bus services; but anyway few people come to Coggeshall for more than necessities. There is one house that attracts all comers, however uninterested they may happen to be in old buildings. This is the beautiful sixteenth-century timber-framed "Paycockes," with its wealth of carving and brick-nogging, as fine an example as any of an influential Tudor wool merchant's home, rivalling even that of the Greville family in Chipping Campden. The house is now in the keeping of the National Trust. Relics of a very different sort of splendour are to be seen at Little Coggeshall, where fragments of a Cistercian abbey are now incorporated in a private house.

My own fancy in Little Coggeshall, however, is for the Abbey Mill, whose white, weather-boarded buildings until quite recently hummed and throbbed with activity. Essex water-mills are usually worth more than a second look, but I think the palm must go to this one, though now its mill-wheel turns no longer and its last miller is dead. There are people who seem to gather to their character all that is most worthily typical of their native home and of their calling: such was Mr Wyatt Appleford, as gentle and wise a miller as ever hoisted sack, and a son of Essex in every pore of him. Even when his mill-wheel stopped turning, and the dust and cobwebs settled for the last time on stone and sleeve and bin, he continued to live in his little white house that looked over the gleaming mill-race beside a garden gay with flowers. He was more than miller, too: a naturalist of distinction (though he would modestly have refused the title) to whom professionals owed many of their notes and observations and who could imagine no better contentment in this world than to sit beneath his willows at evening, watching the small life all about him, or to lean from his window and hear the otters come whistling through the dark. But Coggeshall is indeed a place to breed such men. Its teeming pride is all behind it now – the cloth-weaving, the beautiful carving – and it seeks its pleasure in quietness. Let those call it lethargy who will; I for one am glad there are still such places in the hurrying England of today where the old walled gardens flourish with forgotten flowers, and there is fruit of a quality this can-fed age has no taste for, and where every turn there are old houses revealing a pride in craftsmanship we do well to remember.

The reader who has a mind for unconsidered trifles may like to hear of a rather remarkable family who lived near by at Marks Hall. The church records show that a certain Mary Waters, at her death in 1620, when she was ninety-three years of age, had 367 living descendants – "16 of her own body, 114 grandchildren, 228 in the third generation, and 9 in the fourth." She was evidently a woman of some mettle, too. The worthy Fuller tells us how she was afflicted with a determined melancholy which not even John Fox the martyrologist could ease. "I am as surely damned as this glass is broken," she exclaimed, dashing a Venetian glass to the ground. But the glass, Fuller says, "rebounded again and was taken up whole and entire, being still preserved in the family." Even this unusual happening, however, did not persuade Mary out of her melancholy, "till at last God suddenly shot comfort like lightning into her soul, which once entered ever remained there." Fuller adds that in her zeal she decided to attend the burning of "Mr Bradford, in West Smithfield," where the crowd was so great that her shoes were trodden off her "and she was forced to go barefoot from Smithfield to St Martin's-le-Grand before she could furnish herself with a new pair."

There are many English towns that parade their history more obviously than Colchester does, though there are few with a more interesting history to parade. I do not mean that the city is unmindful of her twenty centuries of recorded story: far from it; but that she lives very much in today – a city of considerable amenities, of beautiful aspect, and of thriving industries. Colchester was important before the Romans chose it as the first colony to be established in this country. Here, five years before the coming of Christ, reigned the British king Cymbeline. And here, sixty years or so later, Boadicea made her fierce and terrible stand against the Roman conquerors. The Normans, in their turn, were quick to grasp the importance of this centre and built here their biggest castle – half as big again as the White Tower of London. And finally, here the Royalists in 1648

endured a twelve weeks' siege at the hands of the Parliamen-
tarians and were finally compelled to surrender for lack of food.
How could such a frieze of proud events fail to leave its mark on
the town? Nevertheless, its most ancient history is today largely
confined to relics displayed in the Castle Museum and to certain
outstanding historical monuments in the town, notably existing
sections of the Roman town walls, the Roman Balkerne gateway, St Botolph's Priory ruins, and, foremost of all, the Castle
itself. It is to the Castle, of course, that the visitor will immediately find his way, for this is the core and matrix of the city's
history. After the 1648 siege, the building, already unroofed and
dilapidated, became a ruin. From being a royal castle for five
hundred years, it passed into private hands and was even
acquired by a local ironmonger, who proposed to demolish it
altogether for the sake of the old materials. This insensitive
citizen did actually get as far as removing the two upper storeys
(hence the dwarfed nature of the Castle today), when bankruptcy fortunately prevented him from completing his intentions. If only all our ruined castles could have been as attrac-
tively restored and preserved from further decay as Colchester
Castle has been. It is indeed a fine tribute to the conscious pride
of the town in its immemorial past. And when the visitor has
had his fill of Roman and earlier relics, he should wander out
into the town again and penetrate behind the main shopping
streets to the narrow alleys and Tudor ways that are one of the
joys of Colchester today. If, as I believe, eighteen hundred
bombs were dropped on the city during the last war, it is
remarkable how little evidence they have left. Some incidentally, that fell on or near the Castle, either failed to explode or
merely revealed by their craters hitherto undiscovered Roman
drains and a Roman road. North Hill, the Stockwell Streets
(including West Stockwell Street, where at numbers 11-12 lived
the family of Taylors, of whom Jane is to be remembered as the
author of "Twinkle, twinkle, little star"), Scheregate, and
Trinity Street are usually considered the most interesting
architecturally, but there is charm too in such little, trafficless
alleys as the Long and Short Wyre Streets. The market, like all
other markets, has dwindled of late; but Colchester remains one
of the chief military centres in the country, and there are
proposals afoot for substantial civic developments in the near
future.

It is an altogether different Essex which one encounters east and south of Colchester – the Essex of the marshlands and estuaries, where half-timbered houses give place gradually to weatherboard, and ploughed land to grazing meadow, and the men of the fields to the men of the sea. It is a district with a life all its own – the secret life of the smuggler so amusingly portrayed in the tales of Mr S. L. Bensusan. For miles inland there is the smell of salt water, and all manner of boats ride as if on green waves of grass. Here is the rich pastureland – the region that used to be so deplored by the old writers for its ague, "that most cruel quarterne fever" which the nineteenth century, with its excellent drainage systems, did much to dispel. Of the many interesting villages scattered throughout this part I can call attention here to only a few; but from Harwich, the port to Europe, to Maldon, with its view over the Blackwater and its mounded silhouette of church towers, there is no part of this countryside without its reward. Tolleshunt D'Arcy should on no account be missed by anyone who has an eye for Regency architecture. It was here that Dr Salter, physician and ornithologist, lived, and Salter Lodge now houses his famous collection of birds. It is here too that the visitor may see one of the few remaining original maypoles in the country. Fenced off among its cluster of hawthorn bushes in the centre of the road, it offers a pertinent reminder of a merrier England, though I for one do not quite see why it had to be topped with an ornate weather-vane. A few miles east, towards the coast, lies Tollesbury, in whose church, by the way, there is a font which was presented, in 1718, by John Norman as a gift of penance for his ill behaviour one day in the church. "Good people all, I pray take care, that in this church you do not swear, as this man did."

But the appeal of Tollesbury is not in the built-up vicinity of the church; it is down by the water. Sea were too definite a name to give to this maze of erratic channels, whose bird-haunted mud holds the sunset like a painter's palette. Here are the boat and yacht builders' yards, where capped and jerseyed men and lads follow their most English calling to the sympathetic accompaniment of sighing plane and chiming hammer. The skeleton of a boat in the making reveals through its ribs the level land-and-seascape where skeletons of other boats in the rotting lie at odd angles in the ooze. And far out on the horizon (or so, at any rate, it was recently) the unwanted ironclads of the last war rust in retirement. When the yards close down for the night, gull-calls and the soughing wind are the only sound. It is a place either of unique and irresistible appeal or of no appeal at all. It reminds me of a phrase in a letter of invitation I once received: "No entertainment given and none asked." For those who incline to the popular notion that the seaside necessarily means piers and brass bands and ice-cream vendors, this indefinable coastline has nothing to give; for it gives what you bring to it – and the gift is transmuted to the pure gold of delight. I have taken friends there whose faint praise could not conceal the extent of their disappointment; but for those who ask not merely the obvious and the full, unequivocal statement, who respond to a hint of mystery when they see it, these marshlands, where early Essex history was made and where today an ancient craft pursues its diminished way, are among the best attractions the county has to offer. For sportsmen, with gun or boat or either, they are almost unrivalled. Even for me, who am neither sportsman nor seaman, their appeal is immense – though if I may express a personal preference, it is for the out-of-season months, when the boat-builders have their yards to themselves and I can have to myself the long sea wall that penetrates far out into these mazy, sea-lavender-lined channels.

Within sight, on a clear day, is Mersea Isle – if island it can be strictly called that is joined to the mainland at low tide by a causeway known as the Stroud. There are many villages in obstinate Essex where some of the families now living can read on the churchyard tombs (and in the parish records) the names of ancestors who were there hundreds of years ago; but perhaps Mersea excels in the number of families who for so many generations have continued to live in the same place. Many of the Mersea families are of French, or perhaps Flemish, origin, and their names, Musset, D'Witt (de Witt), and Hewes, occur again and again in the little island's long history. And one way or another these families are all and always connected with the sea. Oysters, of course, are the place's chief claim to fame and interest, but of this historic and intriguing industry I shall have something to say later. The majority of the houses on the island are of recent construction and little beauty – the inevitable villas and bungalows of retired folk who have a fancy for the sea. But down by the water-front in West Mersea there is at least a compensating picturesqueness in the several original weather-boarded cottages where the smugglers lived, but which now, for the most part, house "the foreigners" of the island. All manner of boats are to be seen here, from the most up-to-date yachts to a conglomeration of house-boats near the Hard, whose occupants live here throughout the year. A fine Norman church, into whose tower many Roman tiles have been built, stands by the Stroud. And in a garden opposite there is an ancient walnut-tree, its wounds filled with cement, its bleached, almost silver bark revealing its enormous age. Of East Mersea, across the island, it is pertinent to remember that the vicar towards the close of the nineteenth century was the Rev S. B. Baring-Gould, who has left, in *Mehalah: a Story of the Salt Marshes,* a novel that is not only a precise and vivid first-hand picture of Essex estuary life in the days of the smugglers but also one of the finest period works of regional fiction in our language. It is the writing of a man who knew this district and this people from A to Z; and if the tale itself is romantically conceived in its plot, in its setting it is severely and appropriately realist. "The sea is not here what it is on other coasts – foaming, colour-shifting, like a peacock's neck: here it is of one tone and grey, and never tosses in waves, but creeps in like a thief over the shallow mud-flat, and battles like a dotard over the mean shells and clots of weed on our strand."

By the sides of the creeks and along what was the high-water mark before the sea-wall was built are the curious Red Hills whose origin is still largely a matter of conjecture. At one time or another bits of late Celtic and Roman pottery have been found in them, but nothing has been found to establish really reliable evidence of their purpose. Here is what Baring-Gould says of them in his *Mehalah*: "Who raised these mounds? For what purpose were they reared? These are questions which cannot he answered satisfactorily. One thing is certain. An immense amount of wood must have been consumed to burn such a mass of clay, and the country must then have been more overgrown with timber than at present. Many of the mounds are now enclosed in fields by sea-walls which hold out the tide, the plough has been drawn over them, and the spade has scattered them over the surface, colouring a whole field brick-red, and making it rich for the production of corn. There is no better manure than a red hill." And here is what the Royal Commission on Historical Monuments suggests as to their origin: "The

material was brought by water, perhaps as ballast, and dumped
at the edges of the creeks to form 'hards' or landing-places." At
any rate this is as plausible an explanation as any that has yet
been offered.

Further east, towards the joyful Clacton where every Essex
cottager aims to spend at least one summer's day by the sea, is
St Osyth, with its twelfth-century Priory, one of the original
forty-seven religious houses in Essex, broken up at the Dissolution, and now mainly remarkable for a magnificent flint-faced
Gatehouse (1488). The Priory was recently sold to the Loyal
Order of Ancient Shepherds Friendly Society and a war memorial to the Essex fallen of both world wars is proposed. It is said
to occupy the site of the original nunnery founded by St Osyth,
who, as daughter of the first Christian king of East Anglia, was
betrothed to the king of the Saxons, an alliance she seems to
have resented to such an extent that she escaped during the
wedding ceremony and took refuge in a nunnery. Later she
founded a nunnery herself, here at St Osyth. But no good came
even of this, for in time the Danes overran the nunnery and
beheaded Osyth. Legend says that she escaped yet again, with
her head tucked under her arm; and where she finally fell a
spring gushed out of the ground and may still be seen (and
wished at, if that is your way) in what is called Nun's Wood.

The district hereabout, in fact, would seem to cherish this
sort of macabre tale. North of St Osyth is the Liberty of the
Sokens, wherein are included the villages of Walton-le-Soken
(otherwise Walton-on-the-Naze), Kirby-le-Soken, and Thorpe-le-
Soken. Many Danish names in the locality testify to the existence here in former times of Danish communities, who, as the
Doomsday Book tells, enjoyed unusual privileges under feudal
law. The word "Soken" is of Saxon origin and implies a district
with peculiar privileges (or liberties) of jurisdiction. In fact,
these Essex Sokens are sometimes called "Peculiars." One of
their ancient privileges still holds: they have a coroner of their
own. But it is not of such technical matters as this that I wish to
write here: the grim tale of St Osyth had reminded me of the no
less grim tale, in its way, of Kitty Canham, a one-time beauty of
Thorpe-le-Soken. Her beauty was her undoing. Although she
was a married woman, she eloped with Lord Dalmeny and lived
on the Continent with him for three years, having married him
at Verona under the name of Catherine Canham. As she lay

dying, remorse compelled her to request that she should be buried in the churchyard of Thorpe-le-Soken. His lordship complied, and one day in August, 1753, arrived there with the embalmed body. In disguise he presented himself to the vicar and told him of the dead lady's last wish. No doubt the vicar was surprised at the request, but he must have been a great deal more surprised when he recognised in the lifeless face the features of his wife. One version of the story says that Lord Dalmeny had concealed the corpse in a trunk, where it was discovered by the excise men, otherwise the vicar might never have been any the wiser. However, the story also goes on to add that at the funeral both "husbands" walked hand-in-hand, so it all seems to have ended as satisfactorily as may be. I do not vouch for this unusual tale, but certainly Kitty Canham's grave is in Thorpe-le-Soken churchyard.

Across the mouth of the Blackwater, on the southern side, is one of the nodal points of ancient Essex history, though there is nothing to see there now but a plain stone building on the edge of the sea. I hesitate to recommend you to go there: where hints and gleams and guesses are all, it is so easy to be disappointed. So let me do my best to describe it and then you can decide for yourself. First it is necessary to go to Maldon and then to take the quiet road, through Latchingdon and Steeple, to Bradwell village. But the pilgrimage does not end at this delightful little village. The road leads eastward and ends abruptly at a farmhouse. All hereabouts is marred today by the untidy remains of an airfield; but the last ugly hangers and sheds are left behind in the farmyard, housing implements now instead of war tackle, and the remainder of the journey takes one across a couple of fields to the sea's edge. And there, gaunt against the sky, with no tree near to soften its stern lines, is the old chapel of St Peter's-on-the-Wall. Into its crumbling buttresses many Roman tiles were worked, as so often was the case where a church was erected on some early Roman site. But the building looks like a rather small stone barn away out in the fields, backed by the level line of the saltings and, far off, the sea. And indeed, for several centuries of its thousand years of history, a barn it was. To get the key it is necessary to cross another field to a tiny cottage where (incongruously enough in that salty, bleak situation) a great vine trails over the wall. Expect no colour and surface beauty, no fine ecclesiastical furnishings when you open the chapel door and enter: the interior is of the same austere appeal as the outside – a few rows of dusty chairs on a rough earthen floor and a dusty table for altar, that is all. The appeal is simple and bedrock. These old stone walls, scattering their dust with every gale, are all its story. Yet what a story it is! For here, when the Roman fortress of Othona had fallen and all its legionaries fled, Chad, the first Bishop of the East Saxons, made a peaceful stronghold of Christianity; and this one-time barn, austere at the edge of the sea, was his cathedral. It is the Iona of Essex; and I for one cannot help preferring that it should stand barnlike and lonely in the sea-blown fields, its setting as severe as its story, its lines as simple as the faith it was so courageously built to extol. A few coins and remains are all that have been found of the Roman occupation here, and of the Christian occupation nothing at all remains but this chapel. At the Dissolution this was despoiled, like all the other great religious houses, and was thereafter used as a lighthouse. From lighthouse to barn was its next strange progression; and then, in 1920, it was restored to its original purpose and is now, however seldom used, safeguarded against any further desecration by being held in trust by the Cathedral Chapter.

Chelmsford, the county and cathedral town of Essex, was also a market-town of considerable importance and some colour until, by centring all farming activities on Whitehall, the present regime rendered Chelmsford and every other market-town less essential in this respect. Whatever there may be to say for the politics of the thing, this seems to me a pity, if only because it has done the Essex farmers out of their weekly excuse for a convivial day with their cronies. Time was not wholly wasted when these gaitered gentlemen stood about the Chelmsford streets or sat somewhat lengthily over their Ordinary at the favourite hotel, discussing agriculture (and other matters) with friends and acquaintances; but I suppose it is not to be expected that such oblique benefits would be admitted by the authorities under the present wholly utilitarian scheme of things; and so it seems that the pleasant usages of market-day will never again be what they were. The emphasis in Chelmsford, therefore, has shifted almost entirely to the several important factories for the production of electrical appliances, ball-bearings, radio, and the like. These are its life-blood. Otherwise the place, though not without its appeal as a town of considerable amenities, including a most excellent library and records office, lacks any particular characteristics. Of the cathedral there is little to say, since most of the original fifteenth-century structure (in the words of William White) "suddenly fell down on the 12th January, 1800," the tower and the south porch alone remaining intact. It was only thirty years before this that Muilman, in his reliable and anecdotal *History of Essex,* made the following observation: "At the west end," he wrote, "adjoining to the belfry, is a vacancy, which seems to have been designed for an organ. ... So necessary an addition would render this place of public worship more completely awful and do a lasting honour to the numerous and respectable congregation." White speaks of an organ having been erected "by Crang and Hancock in 1772" (two years after Muilman's perspicacious remarks), so it looks as if the respectable congregation was duly honoured after all. But White is more specific about horse-racing in Chelmsford than he is about its church; and certainly the Galley Wood Races were famous enough. They were held early in August and were one of the chief annual attractions of the town. Probably the peak of their fame was touched in Charles II's reign, by whom they were patronised. According to White, the races comprised a two-day meeting. "The first day was mainly patronised by the gentry and the second by the farm-workers and local townspeople." Presumably, therefore, he is referring to the first day when he says the races "were rarely wanting either genteel company or plenty of good horses." He adds that the course had "a killing uphill finish." Just outside the town stood Moulsham Hall, the residence of Sir Henry Mildmay, a gentleman who hardly lived up to his name. At any rate, the Chelmsfordians, resenting his obstruction of a right of way through the park, pulled his fences down not once but several times, until at last Sir Henry took the matter to court. He lost the day; and, in a fit of rage, had the mansion pulled down and the parklands ploughed up.

It is a strange and most individual country that lies between Chelmsford and Dunmow – the country of the Rodings and the Easters. One can travel here for miles and never see a house, or at most an isolated farmhouse. It is farming country all the way. Its large, well-tended fields are based on a rotation of corn and roots and their ditches are lined with bat willows (an old industry hereabouts), whose slender grey spires, blown to silver on

the wind, add a kind of melancholy to the uninhabited scene.
There are eight Rodings (or Roothings – some say one, some the
other) and they take their collective name from the river that
winds through their chalky boulder clay – a countryside of
hamlets rather than villages, of thatched and white-washed
cottages, flint churches and scattered farmsteads; a countryside
too of primroses in the spring. The names of the eight Rodings
are themselves a joy to recite. Abbots (or Abbess), Aythorp,
Beauchamp, Berners, High, Leaden, Margaret, and White.
Defoe said of them that they were "famous for good Land, good
Malt, and dirty Roads; the latter in Winter being hardly pass-
able for Horse or Man." Another old chronicler said that they
were noted for "the uncouth manners of their inhabitants." That
their fields are bigger than ordinary is due to the fact that, even
within living memory, many of them have been laid together for
a more economical working.

Of the isolated churches in the Rodings (some of them
nowhere near any present-day dwelling) one of the most attractive is the diminutive Berners Roding church, whose tiny turret
shows like a white dovecote far across the fields. But when I last
saw it the jackdaws seemed to be more in possession than the
people, though I met an old man stretching his lean shanks in
the spring sunshine who told me that "parson ho'ds a sarvice
there 'most every Sunday." Margaret Roding is on the main road
and a very different sort of place from isolated Berners; but even
here the church was locked against me and I had to content
myself with the pleasure afforded by a Norman south door
richly ornamented. The two Easters, Good and High, on the rim
of this most individual stretch of country, are not less rural if
they are rather less foreboding to the stranger. In the neighbourhood there are several large old farmhouses, of timber and
plaster, many of them moated and crowned with a fine cluster of
chimneys; today they are for the most part either converted into
farmhands' cottages or reconditioned into the sort of farmhouse
that centres more on its cocktail bar than on its dairy. They all
probably date back to the days of fifteenth-century Sir Geoffrey
Gate, who seems to have been a person of note here and whose
memory is quaintly kept alive in the church of High Easter,
where a gate is carved on several of the beams.

Of Dunmow, Great and Little, there is not much to be said,
except that the former still insists on perpetrating a travesty of

an ancient and most unusual custom, which anyway belongs by right to the latter. In truth, the ceremony of the Dunmow Flitch, as it was observed here until the last war, was little more than an excuse for publicity and totally lacked the serious intent for which it was originally devised. Harrison Ainsworth, the novelist, was largely responsible for its revival, but in this I cannot help feeling he allowed his romantic zeal to outrun his historical decorum. It had lapsed in 1751 and should have been allowed to remain in oblivion. It is said to have been instituted in the reign of Henry III by the family of Robert Fitzwalter. The applicants were obliged to take the following oath as they knelt on two pointed stones at the priory door.

> You shall swear, by custom of confession,
> That you ne'er made nuptual transgression,
> Nor since you were married man and wife,
> By household brawls, or contentious strife,
> Or otherwise, at bed or board,
> Offended each other in deed or in word;
> Or since the parish clerk said Amen
> Wished yourselves unmarried again;
> Or in a twelvemonth and a day
> Repented, even in thought, any way;
> But continued true, in thought and desire,
> As when you joined hands in holy quire.

Then the pilgrim (as he was called) was carried shoulder- high in a chair through the town, with the bacon borne before him, attended by the friars of the priory and the townsfolk. The earliest successful claimant was Richard Wright, of Bradbourne in Norfolk, in 1444, and the latest was Thomas Skakeshanks, a weaver of Wethersfield, in 1751.

Apart from the Thames, the most southerly of the Essex estuaries is that of the Crouch, and a useful centre here is the little town of Burnham, where pilgrims from the Continent used to land in medieval days to begin their long trek up through Essex and Suffolk to the enormously reputable shrine of Our Lady of Walsingham. Thaxted is said to have been one of their recognised halting-places, and it must have provided a welcome relief from the unvarying peasant routine of work and worship when the motley crowd of pilgrims came filing through the muddy Essex lanes with foreign tongues clacking and strange, alien faces smiling a greeting. Ashingdon itself, a small village some seven miles from Burnham, was a place of pilgrimage, the pilgrims being constrained, so it is said, to climb the hill to the church on their knees. At Rochford, a little further south, another ancient custom was observed until very recently. At dawn on the first Wednesday after Michaelmas the stewards and tenants of the manor met by torchlight and assembled solemnly on King's Hill, where, in a whisper, the chief steward opened the proceedings of the manorial court that had not substantially changed since feudal days. In a whisper, too, the tenants responded to the roll call, and the minutes were written with a piece of coal. Why this particular manorial court should have had to be held at such an hour and in such a manner is not known, but it is certainly curious that it should so have persisted all these centuries.

A feature of Canvey Island, at the entrance to the Thames, is its so-called Dutch houses. These are octagonal cottages of a more or less uniform design, with thatched roofs and one central chimney. They are a quaint reminder of the fact that here, as elsewhere along the east coast of Britain, the Dutch were at one time called in to lend their skill in the art of sea defences. Up to the beginning of the seventeenth century, Canvey Island, which is reached by a causeway over the creek, was subject to severe floods; and so a Dutchman, named Joas Croppenburgh, was offered a third of the island on condition that, at his own expense, he would secure the whole of it with a series of sea-walls. He accepted, and, bringing over a number of Dutch employees, set to work. A little wooden chapel was built for the use of these employees; and the oddly shaped thatched cottages which we find on the island today were their homes. The curious thing is that there are one or two other examples, scattered across the county, of these same Dutch houses: there is one, for instance, at Rayleigh Hill and another at Finchingfield. Could it be that the Dutch workmen set a temporary fashion in freak cottage architecture or did some of them settle with their families as far inland as Finchingfield?

In this same south-eastern corner of Essex is Hockley, which once made an abortive bid for fame on account of the supposedly medicinal quality of its water. (Similarly, a chalybeate spa was started at Witham and a bathing resort "for the elite" at

Mistley; but nothing much came of either.) A hotel, a pump-
room, and baths were built, and the little town forthwith
assumed the fashionable name of spa. Somehow the necessary
visitors were not forthcoming in sufficient numbers, The enter-
prise collapsed – like the pump-room. And the no doubt disillusioned population settled down to their former unambitious
routine.

For the rest, the best of the Essex villages and small towns
in the south are all situated within the orbit and influence of
the Forest. Originally the Forest of Essex (it was later called the
Forest of Waltham and then Epping Forest) extended from Bow
almost to Cambridge and from thence to Colchester; also along
the banks of the Thames. It comprised some sixty-six thousand
acres. Hadleigh and Rayleigh, as their names imply, were early
clearings (leys) in the forest; West Hatch and Fulwell Hatch and
Forest Gate were all gateways into the forest; whilst many other
parish names in the district, Theydon Bois, Woodford, Thorn-
don, Greenstead, Maplestead, Ashdon, Birchanger, Elmdon,
Broadoak, High Beech, Brentwood, Hainhault (originally Hain-
holt), all declare their forest origin. Like other English forests,
this one was subject to a strict and complex rule. There were the
reeves, who branded the cattle, each forest parish having its
own particular markings; the woodwards, who looked after the
timber; the regarders and agisters, who looked after the cattle
and game; and the lord warden, who superintended all. Roe and
fallow deer abounded; and the latter are still to be seen here,
continuous in occupation for very many centuries. No one but
the king and his friends might hunt the deer. Indeed, the royal
gifts of Essex venison make envious reading today. All the dogs
belonging to owners who lived in the forest parishes had to have
their claws cut off their forefeet, close to the ball, to prevent
them from chasing the deer. As for the villagers themselves,
their privileges included the rights of pannage and lopping, of
turning their pigs loose for acorns and beechmast, of freedom to
graze their horses and cows in the glades, and of collecting such
dead wood for firing as they could find: of these, pannage and
pasturage still exist as common rights. But since five thousand
and five hundred acres of the forest were taken over by the
London County Council and dedicated by Queen Victoria to "the
free use of the people of London for ever," the ancient rule of the
lord warden has given place to that of a committee of twelve

councillors and four verdurers and a chief ranger. Any regrets are probably futile, since it is certain that the commoner had very little sensible advantages from his forest in the old days, as the many quarrels and litigations attest. Anyway, the Londoners' Playground it is; and for this the Londoners should give lasting thanks to Sir Robert Hunter, who, as solicitor to the Common Preservation Society (1865), by his strict marshalling of all the evidence brought the many law cases to a successful conclusion and so paved the way for the 1878 Act of Parliament which ordained that the forest should remain open and unenclosed for ever. As yet the new owners can hardly be said to make the fullest use of their beautiful property. After the manner of most townsmen, they seem to prefer to congregate thickly at a few well-known centres, venturing only occasionally into the deep heart of the woodlands, as if they feared that these were still inhabited by wild beasts of uncertain temper. Among the favoured centres are High Beech, for its view; Chingford, where stands Queen Elizabeth's Hunting Lodge; and Chigwell, described by Dickens in his novel *Barnaby Rudge*. With its predominance of beech and hornbeam and silver birch, the Forest is a place of startling beauty at any time, but perhaps especially in the autumn, as even the traveller by 'bus will eagerly testify, speeding through its luminous shade on the main London to Cambridge highway. If he is lucky, he may even be held up for a moment while a mute assembly of deer block the road, as startled to find themselves where they are as he is to see them there. When St Luke's sun pierces the leafless November boughs to light the fallen riot of leaves, there are few wild places in England of greater charm; but to see the forest at its best and most unspoiled one must penetrate north, towards the Rodings, towards Loughton and Theydon Bois, or towards Monks Wood and Ambresbury Banks, whose ancient earthworks are claimed by some to mark the place where Queen Boadicea made her last brave stand against Suetonius.

CHAPTER IV

The People

I. THE ESSEX CHARACTER

ONE of the most obvious expressions of the Essex character, I suppose, is to be found in the dialect of the county. But one is handicapped from the start in this matter because of the difficulty of setting down dialect on paper. One might as well try to set down the songs of the birds. How shall the peculiar and unmistakable intonation he suggested – the *tune* to which every Essex man sings his thoughts? And then again: it would need a new set of vowels and diphthongs to reproduce on paper those subtle variations of sound which come as naturally to the Essex man as leaves to a tree. The best one can do, therefore, is to give a semblance of the actual words and trust to the ear of the reader to translate this semblance into the vital thing itself.

What immediately appeals to the stranger, of course, is the way pronouns are confused in the Essex dialect (as in the dialects of other counties) and the reckless manner in which it makes use of the negative: "I ent seen nothen o' shee for a long while." "That must be gettin' nigh time for we's dinner." Then there is the idiosyncratic and highly effective use of the verb "to do": "He 'ont try that trick many times, do he'll soon hear suthin' about it." So the single word slides into the sentence and by a natural economy is made to do the work of three. I heard of a classic (and I hope authentic) example of the use of "do" in this sense recently. A farmhand had occasion to use his pitch-fork, which he always kept in the barn. He sent a boy to fetch it, but the boy came back and said it was not there. "That's a rum 'un," said the farmhand. "Do that don't that did!" This amusing reply also provides an illustration of the invariable use of "that" for "it." Then again, the plural verb is used regardless of grammatical convention. "She say them owd plums ent no good: they're all buggied." And the past tense is a declension all its own in Essex. "I soo my onions last night." Similarly: hoe – hoo and show – shoo.

The Essex cottager is never at a loss for an expressive adjective. In common speech (the so-called King's English) the adjective is, of all words, the most degraded. A few examples, and often the most unsuitable, are made to do service on every possible occasion, as if the modern mind lacked inventiveness or were too lazy to search for the fitting one. But to the Essex old man, though unschooled, it never comes amiss to find the graphically descriptive adjective. For him a drizzly day is "baingy" – and you *feel* the kind of rain he means; a person with one leg slightly shorter than the other is "bumble-footed" – and you *hear* his awkward step in the lane; a small thing is a "doddy" thing; and an untidy woman is "slummocky." The complete phrase, too, is often immeasurably more expressive than any the educated person might find to use in similar circumstances. To sit down to a meal is "to git up agen the table." Of an old woman who was ill and all but starved by her relatives, it was said: "Well, they fare to eat it all away from her." And I make no apology for quoting again an example which I heard from an old woman who, for all her lack of education, was able to make herself understood with a precision of phrase and imagery which few of her grandchildren could equal. "That put me in mind of owd Susan," she said. "She had but one tooth. She use to fold the table-cloth on it, I remember." The dialect substantives themselves are often very expressive. "Dag" for dew; "mawther" for girl; and the onomatopœic "teeter-ma-torter" for see-saw. "Stop your clanjanderin, do!" says the Essex grandmother to the noisy children. Such words are still being invented today, though they say dialect is dead. "She ent no thicker nor a flimbinine!" was a phrase I heard recently, and there was no sense in asking what a flimbinine might be. And the native has a fondness for confused and telescoped words which I have not heard bettered elsewhere. It was an Essex woman who referred to some cross-fertilised flowers in her garden as "crystallised," whilst her "canopin" was presumably a confusion between canopy and counterpane; but I think her best invention was the "thermogene flask."

What does all this amount to, you may ask, in terms of the Essex character? What would a careful study of the county's dialect reveal of the essential and individualist nature of those who use it? Here I am going to call in the aid of an authority, one who knows his Essex thoroughly and has done much to reveal and safeguard its precious qualities. "In Essex," writes Mr H. Cranmer-Byng, whose too brief pamphlet, *Dialect and Songs of Essex,* comes near the heart of the matter, "in Essex the intimate sense, the prevailing characteristic is a sense of humour, and, to a lesser extent, a sense of guardedness in the attitude to strangers. ... The essential depths for tragedy are absent, but you have in this indigenous, natural sense of humour something equally valuable, something light-spirited and keen, sharp, and self-assured, a savour of the winds that blow about the Essex coast, or the independence that springs from a well-founded sense of assurance. And they are assured, these country folk. They'll tell you they ''ont trouble ter argify wi' yer,' and all these sound and masterful characteristics are mirrored and preserved in their speech."

"Foreigners" inevitably mistake this sense of guardedness in the attitude to strangers for something very near churlishness, and certainly nobody could pretend it is one of their more engaging qualities. It takes them years to accept the stranger in their midst; and all this time his every action will be closely watched, his words sifted, his protestations doubted – and he himself will be exploited right and left. On their side, the natives give nothing away: they have indeed taken to heart the Biblical advice to let one's answer be yea and nay. There is a saying that the best lawyer is the Essex farmhand: he will never commit himself to anything. Farmers come up against this quite a lot. "How much more of that hedge is there to cut, Tom?" "A tidy bit, sir," comes the pat, unhelpful answer. Similarly, willingness is the very last attitude you should expect of an Essex native. Ask an old cottager, with time on his hands and (you would have thought) the need to earn a few extra shillings, if he will do a job for you. "Perhaps I could," he will reply, or "I'll see." Even his invitations, when he does utter them, sound rather more like threats. You go to the cottage of a neighbour on some errand or other and "You can come in," says the good wife; but the inflexion she uses somehow gives her invitation an intimidating sound.

It has never ceased to be a matter of some amazement to me how the cottager (especially if it be a woman) knows everything that happens without so much as stirring from her door: she seems to pluck information out of the air. Nor do the men miss much. They may be standing talking to you, engrossed, as you suppose, in the subject under discussion; but it only needs a cart to go down the lane or a speck of humanity to appear somewhere on the distant horizon for them to stop dead in the middle of a sentence; nor will they proceed until the all-important interruption has been scrutinised to the last detail. Everything that happens in their vicinity is directly and whole-heartedly their concern, and they must suck every drop of honey out of it. To be critical, not to say censorious, is the breath of them all. "Of course, that ent nuthin' to do with me, but ..." thus they pronounce judgment, without (as they imagine) committing themselves; for it is axiomatic with them that on no account must they become involved. Privately they will take sides in no measured terms; but publicly they remain strictly neutral. Perhaps this is no more than a relic from the days when the farmer bought them at the local hiring-fair, body and soul, for a few shillings a week. All this may be history now, but it still serves to condition their reactions to life at many turns. It is supposed to take three generations to change a people's character. I think it will take more than this to change the Essex folk's character. At any rate, "Of course, I know that ent none o' my business, but ..." is as far as they have got in their transformation today.

I have a theory (it will probably be proclaimed fanciful) that the Essex countryman's character owes at least something of its quality to the nature of his landscape. Clay and sky are all – the heavy clay that tears the soles off a man's boots and the wide open sky where he hears the larks singing. And my theory is that just this combination helps to give the Essex countryman his odd mixture of harsh realism and tender poetry. Of the realism I have already spoken. It finds expression both in his actions and in his words: "There never was somethin' for nothin', and that ent likely there ever will be." Expecting nothing, he is not easily disillusioned. The poetry in his character is less obvious and perhaps less common. Yet it is one of his frequent sayings when he is in a good mood that he feels "as happy as all the birds." He watches the rooks wheeling and cawing in the sky: "They're scourin' the kettle agen," he says, basing his poetry, as usual, on the homely things of every day. But for me the abiding example of the Essex cottager's sense of the poetic in life will always be an old neighbour of mine, now dead, who not only thought poetry but also wrote it – or, at least, verse. He farmed his garden, as Essex cottagers used to do. He twined crimson rambler roses up his apple-tree for the joy of seeing them there. His delight in old apples – the rare and almost forgotten Lady Henniker was an example – betrayed a fine palate that had not been dulled. He walked alone, and at night, far afield, loving the stars and the nocturnal stirrings of small life. He loved the snow, too, and was careful to be up in time to see it before man's clumsy foot had spoiled it. And he waited every winter for the first blossomings in a great bed of snowdrops, thick as sugar, before his door. It was of these snowdrops that he wrote the verses I treasure – verses written in pencil in his careful script: "The Message of the Snowdrops to me, E.M."

We get our greatest happiness
    From very simple things,
But if we keep them to ourselves
    They quickly take to wings.
The way to make the best of them
    And gain the greatest pleasure
Is sharing them with someone else
    And doubling thus our treasure.
Today, the second of January
    In nineteen-forty-four,
I found out in the garden
    A great surprise in store,
Snowdrops, those faithful messengers
    Of the eternal good,
Were showing in the sunshine
    And doing all they could
To give me faith that truth and right
    Are always, ever best,
To hold to truth by day and night
    And leave to God the rest.

But the Essex character is to be discovered by other traits than those of speech. It is to be seen in the labourer's slow gait. (Even when he is on his bicycle he rides as if he were taking part in a slow race, his speed being one at which most of us would certainly fall off the machine.) It is to be seen in the way he refers to all other counties but his own – and may be even

the neighbouring Suffolk and Norfolk – as "the sheres," with
something of scorn for all but the native, familiar ways of home.
And it is to be seen, perhaps plainest of all, in those many
habits and fancies and intimate customs which make up the
cottager's simple domestic economy. "The best of us," said
Richard Jefferies, "are polished cottagers." But in acquiring the
polish we have too often lost the essential quality of the cottage
character. Here are a few of the expressions of this essential
quality as I understand it. The pride a cottager takes in his
hedge of quick, rounding its top smooth as a pebble, decorating
it with topiarian fancies. The flowers he tends in his parlour
window – scented geranium, gaudy cactus (for he loves a curious
plant as he does a curious animal), and jenny creeper. The habit
he has of sitting just inside his door on summer evenings,
watching the world go by. The polished shells he puts each side
of his whitened doorstep. The ornaments he treasures on table
and mantelpiece – a pair of chained and spotted china dogs, a
fuzzy castle, a gilt-rimmed fairing or two. And only recently I
heard of a cottager at White Notley who used to keep a couple of
cat-ladders, one on each side of the front door, so that the cats
might climb to the thatch and scare the sparrows off.

Where space is so limited and means so slender, order both
indoors and out is essential; and this accounts, at least in part,
for the trimness and neatness that are such attractive features
of the best Essex cottage. Such neatness ranges from the uten-
sils on the lean-to wall to the faggots piled round the apple-tree
in the bit of backyard. There is an entry, dated 1768, in the
records of the vestry meetings of a certain Essex parish,
concerning the home of a poor widow which consisted of "one
floor, one chamber, one Buttery, and a yarde to sett wood in at
one guinea a year." Such tiny cottages scarcely exist any more,
but the habits they bred still persist. Many a thatched Essex
cottage has a lean-to (the door coming up to the eaves, and even
then one must stoop to enter) which opens on to a little "yarde"
whose chief use is to hold the neatly piled faggots and wood for
firing. But such lack of space – and means – could also produce
less attractive traits and habits, as I am often reminded by the
tales I hear of an old couple who lived in one of the two cottages
which together now comprise my home. Let us call them Jack
and Hannah. They lived in the smaller of the two cottages,
where there was one room downstairs with an open hearth and

a staircase that led directly into the one room upstairs. Jack's tools stood round the walls of the living-room, and in a chest of drawers Hannah kept her week's batch of bread. Jack, it appears, was something of a martinet and a substantial drinker: much of his weekly wage, which I suppose rarely exceeded ten shillings and was often less, he spent at a little off-licence pub called The Kicking Dicky and Hannah was often hard-pressed to satisfy his enormous appetite. "As soon as ever he came in off the fields," I was told, "owd Jack used to sit himself on the stool by the hearth and demand his supper. P'raps Hannah had been making him a pancake. You know: a great owd thing about half-an-inch thick, all dough and fat. 'Give it 'ere!' he'd say, and take it in his hands, and cut it on his knees, like so. He never bothered about a plate. But there, his trousers were that dirty anyway they never let the rain in, so a bit of fat didn't matter. Under the staircase they kep' a pig; and when that was a little owd cad of a thing, I recollec' Hannah made a jacket for it." (The stairs were in the room that is now my study, and somehow I rather like the idea that a dressed-up cad once sniffed and snorted where now Shakespeare and Milton and all the rest of them bide.) Towards the end, Jack grew very shaky on his legs and could only get about with two sticks. Evidently this was Hannah's opportunity to have some of her own back. "One day when they was abed," my informant told me, "they had words over somethin' or other. Anyhow, Hannah basted the owd boy good and proper with her whale-bone corset. Of course, if Jack could a-got howd of her, he'd soon a-given her what-for; but he couldn't!"

Country folk everywhere delight in the practical joke, and of course in Essex they are no exception. What else would you expect, seeing that twinkle in their blue eyes? I remember being told of an old widower and his bachelor son who lived alone in a thatched cottage and who both had a reputation for being rather crafty. Their fellow workmen once decided to teach them a lesson – or was it just for the fun of the thing? Dan and Roger (such were their names) would no more have thought of buying wood for the fire than they would have thought of buying a cat for the mice; and their mates on the farm had a pretty good notion where some at least of their fuel came from. There was a handy pile of wood behind the barn. Accordingly the men bored holes in some of the most likely pieces, filled them with gunpowder, and awaited results. Under cover of darkness the wood duly disappeared. And one evening, when Dan and Roger had arrived home and were sitting on the bench in front of the hearth, frying some kippers for their supper, an explosion blew the two of them backwards and filled the room with soot and ash. But the Essex countryman even carries his love of the practical joke into his work and makes a tradition of it. At threshing, for instance, it has become the recognised privilege of the man who cuts the bonds and feeds the drum to throw back any sheaf that is pitched up to him the wrong way round, so that the pitcher has to fork it up again all the way from ground-level. Similarly, it used to be a custom regularly observed in the harvest field that every harvester who, in loading the wagon, pitched a sheaf over the corner must pay for a gallon of beer for all the others.

Nicknames too are a regular expression of the jocular friendliness existing between men and women of the same community. Any Essex village will yield an astonishing number of these; and the interesting thing about them is that they have sometimes become so familiar, so accepted with the passing of years, that the real name is quite forgotten. Here is a list – and a partial list at that – of nicknames from one small Essex village I know. Bonger, Breicher, Boo, Budget; Compo, Cheddie; Dump, Duffey; Flannelfoot; Glory; Hackney; Jumb; Moses; Nicky, Nobby; Pickles; Rainer, Rufous; Stormer, Stormy, Soup, Sojjer, Strawberry; Tod, Tot, Topper, Tosh; and Whiskers. Incidentally, I think Essex must surely take the palm for the number of its men who were christened with one name and are known everywhere and always and only by another. When some official paper needs signing or witnessing, only then does it come to light that Tom is really Charles or that Ernie is really Albert. And this brings me to another common revelation of the Essex character – though it is one that is shared by country folk almost everywhere. Only with the greatest reluctance can they bring themselves to put pen to paper. There is, I suppose, something irrevocable about the written word. The writer has committed himself. And the past is too full of inherited memory of traps and gins set for the catching of the unwary for him willingly to indulge such an action even today.

And is it not indicative of the quality of the Essex character that nowhere else, unless it be in the other East Anglian counties, does officialdom tread so thorny a way? Nobody knows better how to circumvent the rules and regulations of intolerant authority than does the Essex countryman – especially in the remoter parts of the county. But then the whole of East Anglia was always noted for the daring and pluck of its poachers; and I suppose this is where the present skill has its roots. Poaching continues today, if perhaps less generally and certainly with less reckless hazard; but the same instinct remains, and, in these days of multitudinous restrictions, has even acquired a new lease of life. Essex has indeed excellent opportunities for the poacher: not only inland but all down its several estuaries. The villages nearer the coast abound in smugglers' tales. The Rochford and Dengi Hundreds, the Goldhanger and Tollesbury regions, the whole of the Blackwater and Colne estuaries were the terror of the excisemen. Names still survive to indicate the extensive traffic that was carried on, at one time and another, in silks and spirits and cigars. There is a Brandy Hole at Hockley; there are hiding-places all over Thundersley Common; and it is known that even the churches – Rochford, Canvey, Salcott – were used as hides. Everybody, even the most respectable, seems to have been implicated. (The Rev Woodeford, it will be remembered, thought it quite in order to enter in his diary the many payments he made to smugglers, one of whom he disarmingly calls "an honest smuggler," for tea, rum, silk hand-kerchiefs and the like.) And when did it all stop? The answer is, of course, that it never has stopped – and I doubt if it ever will. Where so exciting a sport, and one withal so gainful, has been practised for centuries, it is not easily rooted out. Even when the profit dwindles to almost negligible size, the zest, the sport of the thing remains. And when, as during the recent war and the continued present scarcities, the profit soars again, the sport gains fresh impetus. Much has been made of the defeated efforts of H. M's. Excisemen to combat the Essex smugglers; and, as with the Essex poachers of earlier times, the secret sympathy of the populace is with them. How the native smiles up his sleeve when he reads in his newspaper of the unconquer-able wiles of the men of the estuaries! Or even of his own friends and neighbours further inland. "Country Wine Racket Beats Excisemen" – so runs the headline, and every cottager chuckles with delight. "The marketeers are doing a very profitable trade in 'home-made' wines and country drinks made and bottled in out-of-the-way barns and out-houses, and so far have not been caught. ... Samples of the wine and mead are of good quality. That is why (says a Customs Official) we think country people who know the technique are behind the business." The gentleman was no doubt quite right in his surmise.

II. FOLK-LORE, FUN, AND FANCY

a. Charms and Superstitions

Certainly there is no other region within a hundred miles of London where superstition keeps so strong a hold today as in Essex. In most of the remote Ends and Greens – and very often in the villages, too – there is living somebody who less than a century ago would have qualified for the status of local witch or wizard and would have been dealt with accordingly by the inhabitants. Of actual witchcraft today perhaps the only activity that comes anywhere near it is that of wart-charming: this is practised fairly commonly and manages somehow to keep within the realms of the respectable and the acceptable. One old wart-charmer of my acquaintance claims to have cured men and women and children from far and near; but I have never succeeded in getting him to tell me how it is done. He is a quiet, wary sort of person; his eyes are cold blue; and I am convinced he is genuine in the claims he makes. Anyway, as a wart-charmer he is a member of an ancient and honorable Essex profession. The famous Dr Culpepper's cure for warts, you will remember, was to rub a black snail over them, nine times one way and nine times the other, then to stick the snail on a black-thorn tree. Another way was to rub them with bean-pods. But my charmer evidently goes one better than Culpepper. He does not ask to see the person he is required to cure, nor even to know any other particulars than the number of warts he has to wish away. Then, to use his own expression, he "works" on them, not continuously but as the spirit moves him.

I would not expect my wart-charmer to have been charged with witchcraft in the old days, however: he is too meek and mild. But you never know. The most harmless people were likely to find themselves ducked in the nearest pond for nothing worse than being a bit different from the common ruck of humanity. Some of the witch trials in "the good old days" achieved quite a notoriety – especially a seventeenth-century

trial of witches at Chelmsford, conducted by Sir Harbottle
Grimstone and other local magistrates. "For the supposed crime
of witchcraft and demonology" (I quote from William White, but
the facts are substantially the same in all sources) "the following were executed at Chelmsford in the year 1645, viz., Eliz.
Clarke and Eliz. Gooding, of Manningtree; Anne Leache, of
Mistley; Sarah Hating and Eliz. Harvey, of Ramsey; Joyce
Boanes, Susan Cock, Margaret Landish, and Rebecca Jones, of
St Osyth; and Anne Cate, of Much Holland." That same year Sir
Harbottle condemned four other old women to be burnt at the
stake at Manningtree, he himself standing as witness against
one of them. The victims of these trials were villagers of the
poor and drab sort, likely to confess to anything under such
torture as they were subjected to. Typical was the case of Eliza
Gooding, mentioned above. "She went to Robert Taylor, of
Manningtree, who kept a grocer's shop, and asked him to trust
her half-a-pound of cheese. He refused, and she went away
mumbling and muttering. The same night Master Taylor's horse
was taken sick: the belly of the said horse would rumble and
make a noise as a foul chimney on fire. In four days it died.
Master Taylor was induced to believe that Eliza Gooding was
the cause – another witch had said as much – and on this
evidence she was ordered to be burnt. ..."

But there have been just as gullible villagers in Essex much
more recently than Master Taylor, and only the law has
prevented them from bringing their victims to the stake. A few
years ago, in the *Essex Review,* Mr Herbert Collar, one of the
best-informed students of the county's lore and customs, gave
some details of a particularly pathetic case he had unearthed
from the local newspapers of as recent a date as 1863. The case
concerned a harmless old deaf-and-dumb of Sible Hedingham,
called "Dummy," who lived alone and wretchedly in a hut
outside the village and who, in order to make himself understood, had recourse to signs and gestures which were taken by
the villagers to be diabolical in intention: he was therefore
regarded with some awe. Anyhow, some sixty or seventy people
were involved in this miserable business, and Mr Collar makes
the astute observation that nearly all of them "were of the small
tradesman class and the agricultural labourer was said not to
have taken a hand in it." The upshot of it all was that one day in
the local pub the old man was set upon by two people, a young

woman who said he had wished an illness on her and a young man who acted with her. Between them they pushed Dummy in the brook, and every time he tried to drag himself out pushed him back in again, with the result that soon afterwards he died. Here is Mr Collar's paraphrase of the woman's statement in court. "Speaking in a peculiar voice, evidently under the spell of a superstitious fear, she stated that the deceased came to her house, spat on her, and told her that after a time she would be ill and she was ill. She had had a doctor twice in one night, and he could not cure her. Dummy wrote up on a door that she would be ill in ten days. He made her ill and bewitched her, and she went everywhere, but no one could set her right again. ... As far as the incident was concerned, she went to the Swan very bad. She went up to the old gentleman and asked him to go home with her and do her good. He would not go. A number of straw-plaiters who were in the house all remarked how bad she was. The old man got out of the house. Some struck him and pushed him into the mud, and did more to him than she did. She begged and prayed him to go home with her, but he would not. She did not deny striking him, but alleged that Stanmer (her accomplice) took him by the heels and threw him into the water. As the result of the trial the prisoners were found guilty and sentenced to six months' hard labour."

And all this, it may be added, took place in a county that has the distinction of being the only one that ever boasted a professional witch-finder. Mathew Hopkins lived at Manningtree in the seventeenth century. He appears to have heard the call to his future vocation one spring day in 1644. "He had seen some seven or eight of that horrible sect of witches (he said) living in the town of Manningtree, with divers other witches of other towns, who every six weeks, in the night (being always on the Friday night) had their meetings close by his house, and had their several solemn sacrifices there offered to the devil, one of which this discoverer heard speaking to her imps one night, and bid them go to another witch, who was thereupon apprehended and searched by women who had for many years known the devil's marks, and found to have three teats about her, which honest women have not. ..." Hopkins thereupon set about organising his hunt (we are told that he "kept a regular pack of witch-hunters," with three horses for their use). His charge was thirty shillings a head. He had a colleague, one John, ingenuously styled "gentleman," and an assistant, a woman, who acted as searcher. He it was who brought about the Chelmsford witch trial under Grimstone, the success of which induced him to carry his activities into neighbouring counties. He excelled in the identification of "special marks" and the significance thereof. He tied the thumbs and toes of suspected persons and dropped them in the pond, applying the unhelpful test that if they came out of the water alive they were obviously guilty. But he came to no good in the end. According to some accounts, his own methods were tried on himself, and, coming out of the water alive, he was pronounced a wizard and accordingly done to death; but according to his accomplice, John, "gentleman," his profession fell into disrepute and so, after writing his famous pamphlet on the *Discovery of Witches,* he moodily took to his bed and died.

I would not say that witchcraft in Essex is quite dead even now; rather, it has gone underground. But superstition is very much in evidence, stalking in the broad daylight. The first atom bomb had already been dropped when I heard my first instance of greasing the nail that has drawn blood; and the old man who casually and quite ordinarily performed this rite, in the north-west corner of the county, clearly thought that the only extraordinary thing about it all was my doubt. "There's a lot of power in grease," he said. Much about the same time a farmer in High Easter told me he had sent a man to scythe down the weeds in a certain meadow – "a wet-day job." In the middle of the meadow the man left a great thistle standing; and when the farmer pointed it out to him, he said he wasn't going to cut that down, for it was a "holy thistle." Similarly, I am sure there are men and women in Essex who still "tell the bees," as I heard them told in Widdington. This superstitious ritual demands that, on the death of the owner of the bees, the hives shall be tapped with the house-key and the information whispered to the bees inside that their master is dead. I believe the strict observance of the ritual demands also that the hives shall be draped with black, though I did not see this done. But the point is that if the bees are not told, they will certainly go away.

As for minor taboos and superstitions in Essex, they are legion, though their observance is of course mainly confined to the old folk. To keep an owl in the house, alive or dead or even in the form of a china ornament, is to invite the envy of malignant fates. (It is equally an ill omen to hear an owl hooting in broad daylight.) One should never bring hawthorn indoors or even, some say, snowdrops. If a robin crosses the threshold, it brings no good with it. No true son of Essex would burn elder wood in his house: he says the Cross was made of elder wood, which not only explains why it should not be brought indoors and burned, but also why it is the one tree that will grow anywhere. A new moon must never be seen through glass or knives allowed to lie crossed on the table. And if mourners should chance to walk in threes at a funeral, then there will be another death in the family before many months are out. But one could extend the list almost indefinitely.

And where, exactly, is the line to be drawn between superstition and medicine? Many country cures, though they seem at first sight nothing but superstition, might very well turn out to be based on a primitive knowledge of the value of natural objects. Penicillin, if nothing else, has taught us to look a little less scornfully on some of the rough-and-ready cures practised by country folk for their wounds and gashes –when they trouble to notice such things. They will search about for a few cobwebs to staunch the flow of blood – and the dirtier the better. Or, failing cobwebs, they will simply daub a lump of dirt on the raw place. They seem immune to microbes. I know an old man who prised out the last teeth in his head with the uncleaned tines of a garden fork. He then rubbed in a bit of salt. In fact, salt, "the savour of life," as he calls it, is his great cure-all. "You barm yourself up too much," he tells his children, in scorn of their doctor's salves and ointments; "all you want is a mite o' salt." And he is well over eighty and still hale.

Herbal cures, of course, were common knowledge everywhere in former times, and I do not suppose Essex had any monopoly in this matter. Patent medicines have driven their use further and further into the background, with the result that the formulæ of these natural cures are almost lost. In any case, they were usually kept a secret and died with their owner. An old thatcher I know was so scourged with rheumatism (the "Old Man," as he called it) that he could scarcely walk. And now, several years after, he walks with only the slightest limp and swears the Old Man has gone for good and all. The cure? A couple of bottles of some creamy concoction which, without any faith in it at first, he was induced to try and which was made by

an old cottager from wayside herbs. Many people, of course,
possessed such secret cures. But one of them achieved something like local fame and should be remembered here. He lived
in the Forest and called himself Dido. When the London County
Council took over, he moved his meagre belongings into a field
at Chigwell. But he remained essentially one of the Forest's
characters, and his story is told in Charlotte C. Mason's delightful book thereon. Dido's speciality was a green ointment which
he made from a fern – one of those ferns, no doubt, which no
longer exist in the Forest. But he also made concoctions for the
cure of whooping-cough, burns, liver troubles and so forth. The
liver, he said, was the body's kitchen and if the kitchen was
allowed to get into disorder the whole house would be upset. It
is said that when certain families in the neighbourhood were
stricken with scarlet fever, he alone would go near them and did
their errands for them. He made a tisane from dried and crum-
bled sloe and hawthorn leaves which he sold to London tea
merchants. He would leave his hut at three o'clock in the
morning and walk to Bunhill Row and then home again to the
Forest in the evening. Besides his hawthorn tea he would take
with him ferns for sale and wild birds which he had trapped in
the woods.

b. *Nonsense*

Of Essex country humour in the general sense I have already
said something; but Essex also has a very special and local
humour which is all its own. At least, there are only a very few
places in England where the same peculiar branch of humour is
still to be found, and nowhere, I think, to quite the same degree
and in the same continuing manner. I refer to the famous
"Coggeshall jobs." But perhaps I had better first explain the
term. A Coggeshall job or, more properly speaking, a Cog'shall
job, is anything that is done so literally and preposterously that
it assumes the nature of a joke, even of a fantasy. To take a
simple instance. A man finds his ladder is not long enough, so
he cuts a rung from the bottom and fastens it on to the top. That
is a Coggeshall job. Or a man who had to get up very early found
that he had only one match to light his candle in the morning,
so he struck it overnight to make sure that it was a good one.
Just why Coggeshall should have been singled out for an excess
of such ludicrous behaviour I do not know; but there always

have been Coggeshall jobs and, what is more interesting, there still are. For miles around this little town any awkwardly executed task is still called a Coggeshall job. "That's a bit of Coggeshall, if you like!" And of the man who thus exposes himself to ridicule it is said, "He's a proper Cog'shall!" It is this continuity that distinguishes Coggeshall from such historical instances of the same sort of thing: the Men of Gotham, the Yawnies of Yubberton, and the mythical natives of Purbright, Pershore, Darlaston, Towdenack and I suppose a dozen other villages where such jokes have fastened like burs on a coatsleeve.

John Ray, who, besides being one of the foremost and earliest botanists in the land, also amused himself by collecting and recording local Essex proverbs, has a rhyme which runs:

Braintree for the pure,
    and Bocking for the poor;
Cogshall for the jeering town,
    and Kelvedon for the whore.

And this was presumably an old saw when Ray mentioned it in 1768, though he is polite enough to add in regard to "jeering" Coggeshall that "this is no proverb, but an ignominious epithet fastened on the place by their neighbours, which as I hope they do not glory in, so I believe they are not guilty of." Guilty or not, the reputation for such nonsensical behaviour sticks to them still. You can even have the cottage in Bridge Street pointed out to you where, when the river rose and began to pour over the floors, the inhabitant is reputed to have cut away the bottom stair to prevent the water rising to the bedroom.

Examples of Coggeshall jobs, in fact, are both many and amusing. Here are just a few. One day the men of the town noticed that their church clock struck only eleven times at noon, whereupon they inquired everywhere for the missing stroke and finally learned that the clock at Lexden, nearby, had anticipated Summer Time by striking twelve strokes at eleven o'clock, and so sent off a horse and cart to bring back the truant stroke. It was the Coggeshall Town Band that provided one of the best of these jokes. It appears that it was practising in an upper room in a house in Stone Street, when somebody came in and told the bandsmen how lovely the music sounded down in the street. To a man, therefore, the band left their instruments and trooped out to listen. Or again there was once an outbreak of scarlet fever over at Kelvedon, so the Coggeshall folk put hurdles across the road to prevent it spreading to their town. When the Coggeshall men volunteered to defend their homes against Napoleon, they were so uncertain of their left and right that the serjeant had to tie a wisp of straw on every right leg and a wisp of hay on every left leg before he could get them to drill properly: "Hay, straw. Left, right!" And was it not the men of Coggeshall who put hurdles across the river to turn back the water? And who chained up a wheelbarrow in a shed lest it should go mad after having been bitten by a dog? Similarly, they forgot to put any windows in their church when they were building it, so they took some hampers and opened them to catch the sunlight, and then, quickly shutting them, carried them inside and let the sunlight out. On the tower of this same church, now unhappily standing no more, since it was bombed in the last war, they one day noticed some grass growing and therefore hoisted up a cow to graze it. At another time, two men, having enjoyed a number of drinks at the Woolpack Inn, decided they did not like the position of the church and would accordingly move it. They pushed and pushed, with no effect except to get themselves very hot, so they took their coats off, laid them on the ground, and pushed again. Then they found they were pushing against the wind, so they went round to the other side of the church and continued their efforts there, this time with better effect. Meanwhile, somebody had removed their coats, so that when they went to look for them, they could not find them. "Dammit," said one of the men, "if we ent shoved the owd chu'ch right over our coats!" And they began pushing it back the other way.

Coggeshall jobs are mentioned in a rambling, queer, ten-thousand-line poem called *The Setting Sun*. It was written in 1871 by a Quaker of Kelvedon named James Hurnard and was recently re-issued under the editorship of Mr G. Rostrevor Hamilton. The poem itself is a highly prejudiced narrative, but it has the quality of being so ingenuous as to disarm criticism, and it is not without interest for any rural East Anglian. Of his marriage with a woman from Coggeshall Hurnard writes:

I caught my bird before I found a cage,
In truth I made a Coggeshall job of it.

And here is his particular version of the hay-straw volunteers:

> There is a town ten miles from Colchester,
> The town of Coggeshall, lying in a hollow,
> Famous throughout the land for "Coggeshall jobs,"
> A town by some folks called the City of Wisdom,
> Of which a number of strange tales are told,
> Blunders absurd and misadventures various,
> Of which I here shall mention only one.
> When Bonaparte tried to frighten England,
> By threatening to invade these island shores,
> The men of Coggeshall, full of public spirit,
> Resolved to form a Corps of Volunteers
> For the defence of their beloved country;
> But none of them would serve as private soldiers;
> All of them wanted to be officers!
> Yet they agreed upon the point of tactics.
> The town of Coggeshall forms a triangle
> With Colchester and Maldon on the coast,
> So they resolved that if the pig-tailed French
> Should make a landing on the coast at Maldon
> Then they themselves would march to Colchester,
> In order to protect that ancient port.
> If, on the other hand, the French should come
> Up the broad Colne, and land near Colchester,
> Then they would march immediately to Maldon!
> So sang the luckless bard of Coggeshall town,
> In burlesque verse, "The Coggeshall Volunteers."
> He was a clever thriving schoolmaster,
> But gave such umbrage to the men of Coggeshall
> By the hard-hitting satire of his poem,
> He lost his school, and so, poor man, was ruined;
> In short he made a "'Coggeshall Job' of it."

c. Customs

Two old Essex customs, appertaining to the Forest and now long since extinct, call for attention here: they are the Fairlop Fair and the Easter Stag Hunt. Perhaps a more appropriate name for the former would be the Fairlop Festival (its detractors even went so far as to call it a Saturnalia), for it had nothing to do with buying and selling and was, in fact, a spontaneous celebration arising originally out of the frolicsome mind of one Daniel Day, an opulent block-maker of Wapping, who was in the habit of resorting annually with his fellow block and pump makers to a monster oak-tree in Hainault Forest, where a suitable feast was spread. Indeed, I would not be surprised if the old oak-tree really had more to do with it than Mr Day. Clearly it was a gigantic tree; and there is reason to believe it was venerated (and even more than this) long before ever Day came on the scene. Gilpin in his Forest Scenery (1791) goes so far as to assert that "the tradition of the country traces it half-way up the Christian era." When he wrote, it was still a noble tree. "About a yard from the ground, where its rough, fluted stem is thirty-six feet in circumference, it divides into eleven vast arms; yet not in the horizontal manner of an oak, but rather in that of a beech." Somehow, Daniel Day's private celebration gradually developed into a regular pleasure fair, held each year on the first Friday in July; and in time it assumed such riotous proportions that the authorities stepped in and discontinued it on the pretext that it had become a menace to law and order. (The truth probably was that, one way and another, it interfered with the amenities of the forest deer, or so one assumes, since its discontinuance was ordered by Lord Tilney and the Forest Verdurer.) Daniel Day seems to have been something of a character. His means of conveyance to the scene of the festival was by boat: three fully rigged model ships, mounted on carriage frames, each drawn by six horses, with postilions and out-riders, and attended by music. Probably the modern interpretation would be that Day was an exhibitionist, though personally I think this a churlish term for one whose flamboyance obviously gave so much pleasure to others. He was evidently generous, too: at any rate, we are told that "in course of time great crowds were attracted, but Day never failed in his hospitality, distributing his stores from the hollow trunk of the oak." A few years before his death a storm blew a large limb off the tree, and, according to his wishes, his coffin was made from this limb and he was buried in it, at Barking in 1767, at the age of eighty-four. Daniel Day was dead, but his soul certainly went marching on. The annual festival grew in size and hilarity, and even its official discontinuance could not completely snuff out the spark he had lighted. The tree became an object of pilgrimage; and when, in 1805, it was finally destroyed by fire (some said by gypsies camping beneath it, but gypsies are always fair game) bits were eagerly sought after and made into all manner of toys and trifles; a part was made into a carved pulpit and placed in St Pancras New Church in London. But let the last word about this remarkable old Essex tree and the folk festival that grew up around it be by John Hanson, who, living for a time in the vicinity, wrote, with a total disregard for punctuation: "This Fair was the resort for many years of the best Company and all the respectable Families for many Miles round furnishing an extraordinary and enchanting scene and was a day exhibition equal in interest and effect to that of a night one of a Gala Festival at Vauxhall but of late years from the excess of disreputable people coming from London and annoyance taking place it has been on the decline and neglected and the old Tree itself partly by Fire from wantonness and partly by the Axe is now completely destroyed and not a vestige of it remains" (1809).

The second Forest custom may well have been, in its heyday, quite as spectacular and even more noisy; but unfortunately there seems to have been very little written about it at first hand and its true origin is lost in a maze of conjecture. The Easter Stag Hunt (or Epping Hunt, as it was also called) was said to date back to 1226, when Henry III confirmed to the citizens of London "free warren" (or liberty) to hunt in the Forest of Epping and Hainault. The Hunt was long attended by the Lord Mayor and Aldermen. The kennels for the hounds and a house belonging to the hunt were rebuilt as late as 1800. The field assembled at Fairmead Glade; the stag's antlers were decked with ribbons; and the beast was usually uncarted about mid-day, to be hunted far and wide. No doubt Tom Hood, in his well-known ballad, exaggerated the motley character of the followers; but altogether the scene was evidently something to be remembered. The hunt became, in fact, quite farcical, however noble its origins: stalls and booths, piemen and vendors were its final excuse. Mention of the Easter Stag Hunt invariably calls to my mind a tale I was once told by the late Miss Anne Tamplin, of Newport. An Epping stag was released at Stanstead and had taken refuge in the Newport churchyard walk. Miss Tamplin's father, who was the vicar and a man of great personality, "drove" it into the vicarage stables, shut it up, and gave it water. It was in an extremely exhausted condition. When the hunt arrived on the scene, the white-haired old clergyman refused to allow the stag to be hunted any more, and after much opposition it was finally taken back to Epping, doubtless to enjoy a less happy experience another day. This, Miss Tamplin said, happened "round about 1890." Somehow that panting stag among the tombs in the churchyard walk has always remained at the back of my mind as typical of the sort of refined cruelty that lay behind the colour and ceremony and tradition of the Epping Hunt.

But the Epping Hunt and the Fairlop Fair are Essex customs that have achieved some notoriety: my own preference is rather for the local customs of a simpler, quieter kind. I like to know, for instance, that the villagers of Purleigh used to greet the May dawn with a hymn sung from the tower of the church. I like to hear how in Rochford they held a cockcrow manorial court where the proceedings were conducted in a whisper and the minutes were written with a piece of coal. There is more than whimsy in such things. They are like those fragments of stained glass, vivid and broken and often unintelligible in their present isolation, that are all some village churches have been able to save from the wild glory of picture and colour that shone in their church windows centuries ago. They are the shreds and patches of our island history, and some of them date so far back there is no knowing when they were fresh and ordinary as the daily task. Such, for instance, was the practice in the Saffron Walden district of carrying round May Day garlands in the middle of which was a doll. I know this was done in the little cul-de-sac village of Widdington until the first world war – the date, by the way, when most old rural customs, however tenacious, were dropped. The villagers did not realise that without a doubt their garlanded dolls were intended as representations of the Virgin Mary ("it was just what we always did") and that their flowery display was therefore a curiously surviving instance of how the Church, in her wisdom, gave the old pagan rite a Christian twist. In the same village the gleaning bell was run as recently as 1912 – as in other Essex villages. For his services in ringing that bell, before the sounding of which nobody might go into the stubble fields and glean, the sexton was rewarded by a collection made among the gleaners, every gleaner contributing a few pence. The bell was rung again in the evening, after which, with sacks and prams and crying children, the gleaners all trooped home.

Harvest customs, in fact, were especially plentiful in Essex. The harvest was contracted out to a team of men, working under a "lord," whose duty it was to set the pace and keep the peace between master and men. Hilman put the matter thus: "He that is the Lord of Harvest, is generally some stay'd sober working Man, who understands all Sorts of Harvest Work (cf. Matt. ix. 38). If he be of able Body, he commonly leads the Swarth in reaping and mowing. It is customary to give Gloves to Reapers, especially where the Wheat is thistly." At the back of most harvest customs was the notion of collecting largess. I suppose they were, in fact, a means of increasing the wages for a service which benefited all; but the collecting of largess often died out before the custom which occasioned it. The most interesting Essex custom of which I have heard, among such that were associated with the work of the fields, was a Plough Monday ceremony which, in certain districts, took the following form. The selected ploughmen, who drew their decorated plough round the parish on the first Monday after Epiphany (i.e. before the season's ploughing began), and who threatened to plough up your threshold if you did not give them money, used to gather in a ring, bend down with their heads altogether, and hum like a bell; and then, at a given signal from the leader, they would all fling their heads back so that the resonant, muffled hum suddenly exploded into a cry for largess.

There were other harvest customs, however, that had no monetary significance, being indeed but a delightful play of spirit. Such was that one, common all over Essex and still kept alive in certain districts, of making corn necks and dollies. Straw is an intractable material and yet there seems nothing which Essex fingers cannot (or could not) do with it, from weaving lovers' knots for buttonholes to plaiting these intricate necks and dollies. The origin of the necks is a matter for conjecture; antiquarians contend that they are really images, stylised female figures, plaited out of the straw of the last sheaf of the harvest and intended to represent Demeter, the goddess of corn. But they are not limited to this particular type; they can, in fact, be almost anything nowadays, from birds to crowns and shapes that have no recognisable analogy at all. Most villages in north-west Essex include somebody among their numbers who is still able to weave or plait these ingenious toys. The best necks I have seen, of the correct, traditional shape, are made at Terling, near Chelmsford; but in Great Bardfield there is a villager who excels in more unusual and enigmatical shapes. There seems to be nothing this Bardfield man cannot fashion out of straw, helped sometimes by a hazel withy or two where the shape needs extra support, or by a strand of wire. Besides the usual shapes, made of wheaten straw and decorated with barley heads, I have seen shepherds' crooks, lanterns, tables, crowns and anchors, aeroplanes and even sets of fire-irons. Sometimes this dexterous labourer will tittivate his toys with bows of horse-braid, red, yellow, and blue, such as the old horsemen used; but this is perhaps a painting of the lily. And how does the maker of the traditional neck set about his task? With a pulled-out bundle of straw at his feet, he will most likely settle himself comfortably on a sack of fertilisers in the barn. First he draws out a handful of the best and soundest straws – for he will only use those that are without crack or blemish. Next he arranges them so that the heads come evenly together. Then he secures the bunch, top and bottom, holding the wheat heads downwards. With the straws he will then proceed to plait his twisting pattern round the gathered bunch, so that it expands slightly in an even spiral, thinning again towards the apex, where a couple of bunches of barley straws are attached, the long tails dangling down on either side. Finally, the whole thing is finished off with a loop of chain-woven straw for convenience in hanging the neck on the nail. He works with incredible speed and rare skill, yet he will tell you that he was never taught: he just "picked it up" as a child, watching others. In olden times the neck was always hung over the farmer's door. Or, as still happens here and there among the quieter Essex villages, it was taken to church and hung among the harvest decorations.

Mention must be made, too, of certain farmhands' feasts which were peculiar to the county. On Shrove Tuesday, for instance, according to Tusser, the labourer, after shroving (or confessing) was allowed to "go thresh the fat hen." Other such farmhands' feasts I have already mentioned. As for the beer drunk by the reapers, listen to old Hilman. "In brewing for Harvest, and in Harvest, make three Sorts of Beer, the first Wort or Strongest, you may put by for your own use, the second or what is called Best Beer, whereof each Man ought to have a Pint in the Morning before he goes to work, and as much at Night as soon as he comes in. If they work anything extraordinary their share must be more: Small Beer they may also have plenty in the Field." I suppose it would have seemed nothing strange to the hardened Essex labourer that the wort, or first and finest brew, should be for the master, whilst he must be content with the small, or last and worst brew. (Is it not they who, today, say to their wives: "Make us a wettin' of tea, missus, do!" – a wetting being fresh hot water poured on used tea-leaves?) In this matter of harvest beer it would seem, from all I have heard, that Hilman understated the case. Certainly the Essex farmhand, with his two-gallon cask slung across his back, loved his beer; and it was a frequent saying here that he would do more for a pint of beer than for five shillings.

It would be pleasant to close this section with a long and appetising list of old Essex dishes, but the plain truth is that the county has no characteristic cooking to boast of. I admit that the cottager has a great partiality for suet puddings; but I admit this grudgingly and in the shameful knowledge that even here he is but showing himself a pale copy of his Norfolk cousin, whose dumplings are so much to be preferred. Then there is a species of bread pudding which is much admired. The pieces of stale and left-over bread are put in water to soak, squeezed out, mixed with a little butter and some fruit, and baked, the resultant dish being eaten either hot or cold. There is also an old-fashioned speciality called "fat pork pudding," in which slices of fat pork are rolled in the usual mixture and baked or boiled according to taste. Sweets, as is to be expected, are neither varied nor original, the only one which could possibly be called an Essex dish being apple cake, wherein the sliced apple bides unhappily between two thick layers of pie-crust. For the rest, the Essex cottager can be guaranteed to ruin any vegetables her man takes the trouble (and such a lot of pride) to grow for her, and she is totally uninterested in what she calls fancy stuff. I find this, I must confess, rather distressing; yet it is also somehow quite right. It is in a nice accordance with the Essex character to spurn any sort of frills and fancies, and those homely dumplings, of which the cottager can never have enough too often, are just what one might expect of a people whose lives for centuries have been close-bound to the clay with no time (or money) for indulgence in high-falutin' culinary notions, and whose forebears, in the lean 'seventies and 'eighties, had to keep their hungry children quiet on "floaters" (a pinch of flour, dipped into the water in which dumplings had been boiled, rolled out like a biscuit, fried, and eaten with a little sugar) while they themselves enjoyed, as a special treat, lambs' tails pudding or (and this more often, because they could get a jugful of blood from the butcher's for nothing) black pudding. A one-time neighbour of mine, now long dead, excelled in the making of pork sausages and took his secret with him to the grave; his name is never mentioned now without the admiring tribute that "he was a wonderful man for mixing a sausage"; and that, I feel, is the finest cook's epitaph any Essex cottager would aspire to earn.

III. CRAFTS AND INDUSTRIES

In these days, when a child of eleven or twelve will bring the corn in behind the tractor, steering its awkward load unharmed through narrow gateways and alongside the rick, it is small wonder that the village crafts are dying for lack of apprentices. William White compiled his exhaustive gazetteer exactly a hundred years ago, and his facts concerning the number of people engaged, in Essex, in rural crafts and trades make sad, instructive reading. Consider, for instance, the village of Finchingfield, in the depths of the richly arable north-west corner of the county. Here are some of his figures for 1848, with some of the corresponding figures for today. In William White's time there were four blacksmiths, as against one (too old for his job) now; three corn millers, a cooper, two wheelwrights and a machine owner (threshing tackle), as against none; seven shoe-makers, as against one; three brick-layers, as against two; two saddlers, as against none; and three straw hat manufacturers and two straw plait manufacturers (which must mean collectors only, since almost all the women cottagers in the village then were engaged in straw plaiting) as against none. Thatchers, for some reason, are not mentioned, though a thatched village in the corn belt could hardly have been without at least one: there is even one today. It will at once be seen from this list that a hundred years ago, Finchingfield, like most other Essex villages, was largely self-supporting – a true rural community in the original sense that it made for itself most of those things which it needed in its capacity as a village drawing its life-blood from the surrounding fields. It had, in addition to these craftsmen,

three bakers, as compared with one today; three grocers and
drapers, three "shop keepers"; two butchers, two pork butchers;
three milliners and a tailor; and even its own doctor, whereas
now he has to be fetched from one of the neighbouring villages.
There were also, as I know, itinerant minor craftsmen, not
mentioned by White and yet essential to the self-sustained life
of the community: men like the glazier, who went about the
district with his panes of glass and parcel of lead slung across
his back, mending the little diamond-leaded cottage windows, or
like the millwright, who, with his mill-bill, chisels, and miller's
staff, travelled from one mill to another, dressing the millstones.
In these cases, of course, the craft has died out with the need. I
know of no glazier, for although there are still diamond-paned
windows in some of the cottages, these are now mended with
putty; and I know of only one millwright, and he turned
farmhand long ago, as one by one the mills in his district were
abandoned to the owls and the bats and the rats.

The same tale of dwindling crafts could be told everywhere.
Blacksmiths and farriers, unless they have had the foresight
(and capital) to convert their forges into machine-servicing
depots, have been driven out of practice as much from lack of
apprentices as from lack of work; saddlers, where they remain,
mostly get their living by cobbling and odd jobs, their fine skill
in leather being frittered away on wooden heels and composite
soles; the millers, all but a very few, gave up the unequal struggle long ago, and the winds they disciplined to their use now
tear the timbers from their mills; and the shoe-makers, whose
boots were made to combat the tug of strong, wet clay, now
never make a boot at all and would not know how to do so if
they were asked. Attempts are made, here and there, to revive
the rural crafts, and sometimes with excellent results; but there
is nevertheless something Canute-like in these endeavours; for
the unpalatable truth is that quality and durability, which were
the virtues of the crafts, are qualities incompatible with an age
of mass production, whose aim is not to provide what is needed
but to make the people need what is provided. Only occasionally
in the Essex villages of today will one find a genuine craftsman
still at his job, either because of some persistent and peculiar
demand in the locality, or (which is more likely, craftsmen being
intense individualists and not easily cheated out of a life's
interest) because of an admirable obstinacy in the man himself.

There is just such a persistent and peculiar demand in Essex, especially in the northern half of the county, for the work of the thatcher. In a region of corn in the fields and thatched cottages in the villages it is obvious that there must be a continual flow of work for him; and yet even the number of thatchers decreases alarmingly and it is altogether exceptional today to find one attended by an apprentice who will presently follow in his footsteps. Like the miller from his hatch, the thatcher from his ladder watches the village below and enjoys as much as he chooses the company of the passer-by; like the miller, too, he watches the weather with a narrow eye, though the wind that makes the miller put on more power sends the thatcher home. For many weeks after harvest he is to be found on the farms thatching the ricks, and the householder with a leaky thatch can whistle for him in vain. It is usually just about the beginning of spring when he turns up, dumping his load of straw all over the awakening garden. He expects to be provided with the straw and also with the ladder. For the rest, his tools consist of a short-handled, long-toothed rake, for smoothing the straw and combing out the tangles; a wooden beater, for patting it down; a pair of shears, for tidying the edges; a cradle, or greip, for carrying the straw up to the roof; and a pair of knee-pads. If he is making a totally new thatch, he will also require two big needles, for sewing the straw to the rafters, and some tarred string. Since it becomes rarer every year for a new house to be built with a thatched roof, it is not often that one has the opportunity to watch the whole process of thatching: what one usually sees is a new "coat" being imposed upon an old "waistcoat." The waistcoat is the first thatch and is attached directly on to the rafters, sewn on, in fact, with needles and string. Two men will be required for this operation, one on the roof and one under it, each in turn passing the needle through the straw to the other. In old timber-framed houses where the bedrooms are open to the roof one may see the ends of the string where it has been fastened on to the rafters. This waistcoat is about a foot thick. The coat itself is secured to the waistcoat by the means of hazel spics. And the whole process begins at the eaves, the thatcher working upwards to the ridge, where the straw is bent over, half on either side.

An Essex rural craft which most people find of special appeal, though it is now practically extinct, is straw plaiting. It

is true that other counties practised it, particularly Bucking-
hamshire, Hertfordshire, and Bedfordshire. But in the north-
west corner of Essex, including the villages of Great and Little
Saling, the Yeldhams, the Bardfields, the Maplesteads, the
Hedinghams, Finchingfield, Pebmarsh and Pattiswick, it flour-
ished to quite an extraordinary degree, more than three thousand cottagers being employed in it (not to mention the children) when the trade in straw plait touched its peak of produc-
tivity round about 1875. Moreover, only in Essex have I heard of
a regular practitioner who is still alive, Miss Hannah Freeman,
of Finchingfield, now in her 'nineties. Straw plaiting was surely
the village craft par excellence: those thousands of cottagers,
weaving their straw as they sat in the doorway of a summer's
evening or as they strolled in lane or field, gossiping with
friends and neighbours under an English elm, were the counter-
part of those spinners in the sun as they are still to be seen
every day among the vines and fig-trees of France, Spain, or
Italy. It is said that the craft was first introduced into the
county at Gosfield, by the Marquis of Rockingham, about the
year 1700. If this is so, then its growth and development at first
were very slow; for, although Arthur Young, writing in 1805,
praised it as one of Essex's "greatest temporal blessings," the
census of 1851 revealed that only some fifteen hundred people
here were employed in it. In fact, as a country craft of prosperous proportions it enjoyed a comparatively short life, though it
lingered on until well into the 'nineties or even later. When it
was at its peak, straw plaiting would bring as much wages to
the women, working so to speak in their spare time, as their
regular job did to the men working from dawn to dark on the
farms; and even little children could earn good money at it. Miss
Freeman recalls, for instance, that her mother used to allow her
to get up especially early on Sunday mornings to plait, when she
was a little girl, and that "we were allowed to have the money
we earned to buy pinafores." Miss Freeman has told me in detail
how straw plaiting was done; but as I have set down her story in
another place, I will content myself here with the barest outline
of the work involved.

The cottager usually bought bundles of straws already
stripped, i.e. cut just above the knot to a length of nine or ten
inches, from a dealer, though sometimes the straw was grown in
the back garden. The straws were bleached by being placed in

an old tin or box into which lighted sulphur had been lowered. Suitable straws were then selected and split on a tiny bone or steel "engine" either into three, four, and so on, up to ten, "splints." These engines were neat little contrivances whose several blades radiated from the pronged centre like spokes from a hub. By inserting the prong into the open straw end and pressing hard with the thumb, the straw would be split into the required number of pieces. These had then to be rolled in a mill, which was usually kept nailed against the wall. When wetted, the splits were tied into loose bundles and tucked under the arm, and the work was ready to begin. There were many species of straw plait, of varying complexity of design, and payment was made accordingly. The most popular plait in Essex seems to have been the Double Whipcord, made from seven straws double. There were also One Notch, Double One Notch, Two Notches, Three Notches; Shortcake, with nine straws, sometimes more; Diamond, thirteen straws; Brilliant, perhaps the most delightful and certainly the most complicated (and therefore the most highly paid) of them all, the number of straws in this design ranging from eight to as many as twenty-four. (For home use, such as the making of those flail baskets in which country folk used to take their food into the fields, a simple straw plait called Wisp was used.) The finished article was made up into lengths of twenty yards ("scores") and wound round a half-yard board to simplify the counting when they were taken each week to the local dealer. This was usually one of the village shopkeepers, who in turn conveyed the week's output to Dunstable or Luton to be made into hats. Most Essex villages had straw plaiting schools, as they were called, perhaps a small room in a cottage, where, with inadequate light and heat, the children were taught the craft even at the early age of four and five; but these schools – the one blot on this otherwise so admirable rural craft and industry – were closed by the Education Act of 1870. It was finally the machine, together with the admittedly inferior quality of English wheaten straw as compared with the Italian, which drove straw plaiting out of existence here.

I suppose this particular craft was to Essex rather what lace-making was to Northamptonshire. And I confess I find something fitting in the county's choice, not only because straw is the native material but because the rougher beauty of straw plaiting is more in keeping with the Essex character. Long before the Marquis of Rockingham (if report speaks true) persuaded his wife to go to church one Sunday morning in a new-fangled hat of woven straw, to encourage the craft among the Gosfield villagers, the Essex folk had been past-masters in the art of disciplining this intractable material to the most delicate uses. I have already mentioned their dexterity in making corn necks and dollies and buttonholes, and to these must be added the toys with which they delighted to ornament the finished corn ricks and the sleight-of-hand bonds with which they bound the sheaves in the harvest field. Certainly straw is their most inevitable material; and perhaps that is why I have never felt the enthusiasm that others feel for the laces made at Coggeshall. This little town is the only place in Essex where it was ever made, and it still is made there, though the craft is but a glimmer of its former self and might at any moment be blown out altogether were it not for the enthusiasm of certain people in the locality. Coggeshall lace-making, however, is in any case somewhat of an upstart in comparison with the more general straw plaiting. It seems to have been introduced into the town by a Frenchman, who, with his daughters, settled there in the early part of the nineteenth century. (Seven lace-makers were listed by White in 1848.) It is called tambour lace, the name deriving from the fact that originally the frame upon which it was made somewhat resembled a tambourine; but nowadays a different sort of frame is used. Coggeshall is the only place in England where this particular sort of lace, made on a foundation of net, is manufactured, and I suppose it is a commendable endeavour that strives to keep the craft alive; but for all that, it seems to me to serve little more than a private purpose. My conviction (or is it prejudice?) is only strengthened when I read in the Coggeshall lace-makers' prospectus that "table mats, D'Oyleys, fichus and fans" are among the articles kept in stock.

But then it is fast becoming axiomatic today that folk crafts, where they persist, have almost nothing to do with the folk. I cannot see Essex farmhands' wives flaunting a fichu or a fan of Coggeshall lace, even if they could afford it; just as the very last kind of pots they would buy are those which are thrown in some of the local village potteries. I suppose one of the last of the genuine Essex folk potteries, really supplying a local demand, was the one at Gestingthorpe. White gives the name of the

potter there in 1848 as Eliz. Rayner, " earthenware manufac-
turer." If this is correct, it may very well have been he who
numbered among his pupils a young man destined to become
one of the county's best-known potters – and a "character" as
well. For there is evidence that Edward Bingham, who set up
his own potteries at Castle Hedingham nearby, was already well
established soon after the middle of the century and by 1875
had even achieved quite a fame. The last potter at the Gestingthorpe potteries (Pot Kiln Chase), before they were closed
down in 1912, was George Finch. They have recently been re-
opened, thereby reviving a craft which had been practised in
this village since the seventeenth century. (Incidentally, the
best Essex tiles – and Essex was famed for its tiles – were made
here.) Edward Bingham is still remembered vividly in Castle
Hedingham, for he was an individualist of the first water, a man
of great integrity and an iron determination to do only the best.
His pottery, which ranged from dairy pitchers and pots and
pans to "puzzle jugs," from plain household ware for the many to
ornate vases for the few, was to be found in homes all over the
district. Some of it may still be seen. There is quite a collection,
for example, in the possession of a local shopkeeper, and most
Essex-lovers have managed to get hold of a piece or two for
sentiment's sake. Bingham sold his ware for ridiculously low
prices, sharing with so many of the genuine old-time craftsmen
the uncommercial notion that honest appreciation was better
than pence. His works were away up an alley off the main street
of Castle Hedingham, and an existing photograph shows him
seated at his wheel, a bowler hat on his head and the traditional
calm and concentration of the craftsman plain on his bearded
face. His pots were characterised by a beautiful glaze and by a
queer and individual ornamentation in which the folk and the
classical elements were ingeniously mixed. He was a member of
the Plymouth Brethren and lived only for his religion and his
craft. Mr Alfred Hill has given a lively picture of him. "He
thought and dreamed of nothing else (but his pots) except on a
Sunday, when he took the train to Halstead, for a meeting of the
Plymouth Brethren in their little chapel in the Bull yard, and
walked five miles back." He was never seen without his bowler
hat and his umbrella. He exhibited his wares in some show-
cases up the alley leading to his works: "like rabbit-hutches on
posts," says Mr Hill.

It is only to be expected that a county so rich in river estuaries and waterways should excel in waterside crafts and marine industries; and of these one of the chief, as it is also one of the most ancient, is that of oyster breeding. There are several centres of this highly specialised and historical industry, ranging from the Crouch in the south to the Blackwater in the north; and controversy is rife among the connoisseurs as to which breed of oyster is best, Mersea or Whitstable, Colchester (which is really Wivenhoe, in this connection) or Burnharn. Essex oysters have of course been famous from the dawn of our island history. The Romans seem to have had an appetite for them that amounted to a passion: even in Rome itself shells of an unmistakably Colne-river character have been found, whilst it is doubtful if there has ever been any excavation work carried out on important Roman sites in this country where dumps of oyster shells, discarded from the Roman kitchens, have not been discovered. The culture of the oyster is nothing less than a fine art, requiring as much expert (and traditional) knowledge as is required in the culture of the French vine. This knowledge, like the oyster beds in which it is practised, is passed on from father to son, the same family often having a zealously guarded reputation through several generations. Such a traditional oyster-breeder is Mr Stoker of Mersea. I remember calling on him one blustery Sunday evening in autumn. Unfortunately he was out in his smack; but Mrs Stoker almost atoned for my disappointment. With a pea-green cardigan clutched round her head, so that strands of white hair fringed her forehead, she led the way up the garden, to where, under a dripping apple-tree, stood the muddy tin basins containing all that remained of the day's catch of natives and Portuguese. Mrs Stoker said she always ate some last thing at night, but her husband would not touch them. "You know how it is," she said; "he's always among 'em and so I suppose he don't fancy 'em." I came away with a bag of natives, but I think I was even more pleased with a good Essex word which Mrs Stoker had thrown in as it were for make-weight. Telling me how she liked to eat her nightly dozen, she said: "Plenty of vinegar on the plate and then – well, I just *scroffs* 'em!"

The oyster smacks go out in the early morning, dredging for cultch, that is, the marine rubbish, including pebbles, oyster shells and so forth, to which the spawn or spat attaches itself.

This has to be sorted out, the rubbish being thrown overboard and the brood put into the beds to mature. These beds are oblong pools in the sand of the river, some five feet by fifteen, enclosed in boarded sides and fairly shallow. They are exposed at low tide and covered at high tide. Defoe, like so many journalists, was not always scrupulous as to his facts; but he was at least vivid. Here is part of an account he quotes in his *Tour of Great Britain* (1748) of the Essex oyster industry: "In the month of May the oysters cast their spawn, which the Dredgers call their Spat. It resembles a drop of Candle Grease and is about the bigness of a Halfpenny. The Spat cleaves to Stones, old Oyster Shells, Pieces of Wood, and suchlike Things at the Bottom of the Sea, which they call Cultch. After the Month of May it is Felony to carry away the Cultch, and punishable to take any other Oysters, unless it be those of Size, that is to say, about the bigness of an Half-Crown piece, or where, the Shells being shut, a fair Shilling will rattle between them. ... This Brood, and other Oysters, they carry to Creeks of the Sea, at Brickelsea, Mersea, Lagno, Faringrego, Wyvenhoe, Tolesbury and Salt-Coase, and there throw them into the Chanel, which they call their Beds, or Layers, where they grow and fatten; and in two or three Years, the smallest Brood will be Oysters of the size aforesaid. Those Oysters, which they would have green, they put into Pits about three feet deep in the Salt-marshes, which have overflowed only at Spring-tides, to which they have Sluices, and let out the Salt-water until it is about a Foot and a half deep. These Pits, from some Quality in the Soil cooperating with the Heat of the Sun will become green and will communicate their Colour to the Oysters. ... To prove that the Sun operates in the Greening, Tolesbury Pits will green only in Summer; but, that the Earth hath the Greater Power, Brickelsea Pits green both Winter and Summer; and, for a further proof, a Pit within a Foot of a green Pit, will not green; and those that did green very well in time lose their quality. The Oysters, when the Tide comes in, lie with their hollow Shell downwards; and, when it goes out, they turn on the other side. They remove not from their Place, unless in cold Weather, to cover themselves in the Ooze. ... The Oysters are sick after they have spat, but in June and July they begin to mend, and in August they are perfectly well. The male Oyster is Black-sick, having a Black Substance in the Fin: the Female, White-sick (as

they term it), having a Milky Substance in the Fin. They are
salt in the Pits, salter in the Layers, and saltest at Sea." And
finally, just as a reminder of the days that will never come
again: Arthur Young reported in 1807 that Mersea oysters were
"sold by the tub of two bushels; generally from 4s. to 6s. [four to
six shillings = 20p-30p] a tub."

Another Essex industry which is almost as old as oyster
breeding is cloth-making, which at the peak of its prosperity
coloured the whole work and life of the townships in the north of
the county and which, at its close, left as a rare legacy the finest
of the Essex churches and no negligible share of its lovelier
houses. Of the chief cloth-making districts of Essex Fuller
wrote: "It will not be amiss to pray that the plough may go along
and the wheel around so (being fed by the one and clothed by
the other) there may be, by God's blessing, no danger of starv-
ing." The reign of Edward III may be said to have witnessed the
beginnings of this great industry, since, prior to that, Essex, in
common with the remainder of East Anglia, had followed the
practice of exporting its fleeces to the Continent, where the wool
was made up as cloth, and then of importing this back into the
country as a finished product. Edward III, however, set an
embargo upon the export of fleeces, with the result that "as the
wool ceased to go to the weavers, the weavers came to the wool."
The impoverished weavers of such Netherland towns as Bruges
came over to this country in an attempt to retrieve their
fortunes – the unwitting vanguard of a much bigger and more
influential invasion later on. The chief wool trade in Essex then
was the weaving of the old broadcloth (broad white cloth) which
continued until the arrival here of the Protestant refugees from
the Low Countries who had been driven to seek shelter from the
religious persecutions to which they were subjected at home.
Altogether some hundred thousand Flemings and Walloons
came to this country, no small proportion of them settling in
such towns as Colchester, Braintree, Bocking, Halstead, and
Coggeshall. These refugees brought with them a skill of such
cunning and an industry of such integrity that, despite inevitable opposition, they succeeded in raising to a quite extraordinary degree of excellence the status of the wool manufactory of
this country. For whatever cause, many of these admirable
settlers were presently to leave England, this time to found new
homes across the Atlantic. Many an Essex place-name – e.g.

Braintree, Dedham, Hedingham, Toppesfield, Wethersfield, etc. – is to be found in New England, a fact that was not forgotten during the last war, when American soldiers and airmen, finding themselves stationed in East Anglia, were entertained by their "parent" town or village. The captain of the *Mayflower* was an Essex man; one of the Pilgrim Fathers came from Braintree and another from Ockendon. Indeed, it has been estimated that, of those early New England settlers, at least half can he traced, either directly or indirectly, to Essex; and the New England dialects contain several words peculiar to Essex.

The main contribution of these Flemings and Walloons to the woollen manufactures of Essex was the introduction of bays and says, "the New Draperies," as they were called; the old broadcloth, which had hitherto been the staple trade, thus giving place to cloths which were typified by the Sudbury baize of Suffolk and the Colchester says, or serges, of Essex. The Essex equivalent to the Sudbury baize was the Coggeshall, or Cog'shall, manikin. In fact, the reader who is curious to know about such things may here like to see the list, compiled by Miss Eileen Power from original sources, of the various cloths included under the heading of the New Draperies. They were: Arras, bays, bewpers, boulters, boratoes, baffins, bustyans, bombacyes, blankets, callimancoes, carrells, chambletts, cruell, damask, frisadoes, fringe, fustyans, felts, linsey-woolseys, minikins, mountaines, perpetuanas, rashes, rugges, russells, sattins, serges, sayes, tulles, tamettes, tobines, and valures. Not much is known, however, about the exact nature of these cloths, except that they required long, combed wool, whereas the old broadcloth had been made from short, combed wool.

The refugees were of exceptionally high character, being reported as "a very honest, godly, civil and well-ordered people." They kept themselves to themselves, forming a distinct colony in the towns where they settled, caring for their own poor and needy, and worshipping, in a church specially assigned to them (St Giles, in the case of Colchester), after the Lutheran manner. Their credit was such that, contrary to the accepted practice, their bales of cloth were purchased without the seals of the sacks being broken, it being unnecessary to test the contents for accuracy of measure and for good quality. Nevertheless, as is usual at such times, complaints began to pour in against the refugees. Skelton, who was Poet Laureate when the first of the

Netherlanders began to arrive, groused against them in the following lines.

> So many Easterlings,
> Lombards and Flemings,
> To bear away our winnings
>   Saw I never;
> By their subtle ways
> All England decays,
> For such false Januarys [Genoese]
>   Saw I never.

Later, in the reign of James I, the English weavers of Colchester protested to the Privy Council; but it seems the protests should have come from the other side; for in 1588 there were even proven cases at Halstead of the Flemings' seals being counterfeited. Such incidents, though unfortunate, probably did not amount to much. In any case, the plain truth was that this infusion of new blood brought fresh life to the industry in Essex as elsewhere. This prosperity suffered its first severe setback during the Napoleonic Wars, when for the time being exports ceased. In the neighbourhood of Colchester, for instance, where hitherto twenty thousand people had been employed in the industry, now there were only eight thousand. At Halstead and Bocking the rates rose to over twenty shillings in the pound. This setback was, in fact, the beginning of the end. Arthur Young in 1807 wrote of the woollen trade in Essex that "from time immemorial it has taken the lead in this county; but from its continuing dwindling conditions, it is uncertain whether it will many years remain so." But by the middle of the century it had almost died – killed by the Industrial Revolution.

A word or two should be said as to the manner in which the wool industry was constituted in Essex. The feudal system had ordained that all workers, in whatever trade, should be bound by the ordinances of their several guilds – the medieval equivalents to the modern trade unions. But the wealthy and influential wool merchants of the New Draperies conducted their business on the "outwork" system, whereby the various craftsmen, spinners, weavers, dyers, carders, etc., worked in their own homes but under the direction of the merchant. Such a system, admittedly, assured that the workers were, at least nominally, their own masters; it also enabled the merchants, especially the more unscrupluous of them, to make immense profits: for one thing, they could buy their wool in vast quantities at low prices and then deliver it to the workers to spin and weave and dye at stipulated and very inadequate prices. The average earnings for spinning and carding, for instance, in skilled and industrious hands were about tenpence a day. It throws a cruel light on the times to learn that the spinning and carding of wool for baize "often very coarse, and saturated with oil, was very troublesome; and from the latter circumstance, and for children especially, probably unwholesome: the combed wool, which always makes the warp of the baize, was much easier spinning, but not quite so profitable." The wool merchants, in short, were capitalists; but they differed at least in one respect from those of the Industrial Age that followed: they showed the very best taste in the churches and domestic buildings upon which they lavished their wealth. How exquisite was their taste in these matters may be seen by anybody who cares to avail himself of the offices of the National Trust and pay a visit to Thomas Paycocke's splendid home in Coggeshall. Paycocke was a Wool merchant who might more fitly be called prince. Actually, the Coggeshall house was built by Thomas's father, John Paycocke, as a wedding present for his son. The name of Paycocke is still kept alive in Coggeshall (where there were families of this name continuously for more than a hundred and fifty years) by other means than the presence there of this magnificently carved old house on the outskirts of the town. The proceeds of a Paycocke charity are still distributed to the poor, year after year; and, as the mighty merchant directed in his will and testament, there are Paycocke scholarships at the Hitchin School.

If the Industrial Revolution dealt the Essex wool trade its final death-blow, it also provided the county with an alternative livelihood in the manufacture of agricultural implements, which now increasingly began to come into demand. Also, early in the nineteenth century a fine silk industry sprang up in some of the centres hitherto given over to the manufacture of woollen cloths, such, for instance, as Braintree, Bocking, and Halstead. Indeed, I suppose the manufacture of silk in Essex may be said to be sequential to the manufacture of woollen cloths, not only for its similarity but also for the fact that it became concentrated in the same area and because it too was pre-eminently the result of the Protestant invasion of this country.

George Courtauld, who in company with other Huguenot families fled from persecution to this country in the seventeenth century, was the founder of the Essex silk industry. Many of these Huguenots were, besides being wealthy, men of taste and erudition, and altogether a most invaluable addition to the population. (Peter Muilman, from whose anonymously printed *New and Complete History of Essex* I have several times quoted, was a Huguenot who lived at Kirby Hall in Castle Hedingham, and a plate of that house is described in the text as being the property of "the present worthy owner and occupier of this estate; but this donation is very small comparatively to his ardent assistance in this undertaking; as through his interest many other copper-plates, as well as several interesting anecdotes and intelligences have been procured; and from an indefatigable zeal of serving this county he is daily adding to his already innumerable favours.") It was in 1798 that George Courtauld launched the business which has since become world famous; but his first attempt to establish the manufacture of silk was not made until 1810, at Braintree. The rapid development of this industry in north Essex, since the introduction of crape (a crimped silk gauze) and the subsequent discovery first of "artificial" silk and then of rayon, completed the fortunes of the firm and rendered the name of Courtauld the modern equivalent of Paycocke in the district. Among other firms engaged in allied branches of this industry mention must be made of Messrs Warner and Sons, also of Braintree, weavers of silk and velvet, whose looms made the Coronation Robe for King George and Queen Elizabeth. Apart from silks, velvets, and so forth, Essex industries today centre, as would be expected, on the county's intensive agriculture. Messrs Bentall's iron foundries at Maldon, and others, provide agricultural implements; fertilisers and farm foodstuffs come from Messrs Cramphorn of Chelmsford and Brooks of Mistley; the Tiptree jam works of Messrs Wilkin are known far afield; there are farmers' millers at Rochford and elsewhere; whilst Messrs Benskins of Watford offer a pertinent reminder that Essex has not forgotten how to brew good beer if it has forgotten to grow the hops for it. Last, but by no means least, there are the Ford Works at Dagenham to carry the skill and labour of Essex men to wherever tractors are used.

IV. A Scroll of Essex Worthies

a. Artists, Writers, Musicians

Modern artists have been quick to avail themselves of the opportunities Essex offers for their skilful exploitation of its subtle lights and spacious scene. Especially have they been attracted to the north-west corner of the county, where, in Great Bardfield, for instance, several well-known artists have established themselves since the 'thirties, the most notable among them being Edward Bawden and John Aldridge. But perhaps it was Sir George Clausen who, among modern painters, first "discovered" this part of Essex and made it peculiarly his own in paintings which are to be seen in most of the major art galleries here and abroad. Earlier still, of course, there was the precedent of John Constable, who found in the countryside around Dedham the substance and poetry of many of his famous pictures. Admittedly, Constable was not, strictly speaking, an Essex man: he was born at East Bergholt, a mile or two over the Suffolk border. In his early formative years, however, when his genius was in the making, he certainly harvested as many impressions in the one county as in the other. "These scenes," he said, "made me a painter"; and it was to the countryside of the River Stour, the boundary between the two counties, that this out-and-out countryman was referring. I like, too, what the Hon Andrew Shirley says of him in his admirable study: "No other painter smelt the land or felt it through his boots in this way." That surely is how one would expect an Essex man to paint!

Constable was the son of a well-to-do miller, a fact which is relevant to our appreciation of his work. Who, better than a miller's son and an East Anglian miller at that, would have acquired such an intimate and specialised knowledge of the clouds and weather? He remained in his father's business until he was nineteen years old (1795) and no doubt his occupation at this time had much to do with his future extraordinary ability in the delineation of the English skyscape. Indeed, his affection for the old mill and for the scene which it dominated found direct expression in his letters as well as in his canvases. "The sound of water escaping from mill-dams, willows, old rotten planks, slimy posts and brickwork – I love such things." But this ardent appreciation of the country scene in no way helped the youth in his pursuit of the miller's calling: it possibly hindered him quite a bit; in any case, his father was finally persuaded, in 1799, to allow the lad to go to London, where he might study at the Royal Academy Schools. All the time he had been at the mill he had been painting whenever possible, mostly from nature, and often in the company of the village plumber and glazier, John Dunthorne, who today is remembered for his friendship with Constable if not for his own paintings. It was to Dunthorne that Constable wrote, after he had gone to London, "This fine weather almost makes me melancholy; it recalls so forcibly every scene we have visited together. I even love every stile and stump, and every lane in the village, so deep rooted are early impressions."

Among the patrons who helped Constable in those early years were Sir George Beaumont and the Rev John Fisher (who afterwards became Chaplain to the Bishop of Salisbury, whose cathedral Constable was to make the subject of one of his most glowing and lovely pictures); and Leslie, the painter's biographer, tells some instructive tales of visits paid to the former wealthy amateur at his home in Cole-Orton. Once, for instance, Sir George, who was very attached to the sombre hues of the Old Masters, recommended to the young artist that he should take the tone of an old Cremona fiddle as his ideal, to which Constable replied by laying the fiddle on the vivid green lawn in front of the house. Sunshine, in fact, was as present in his pictures as it was in Richard Jefferies' books, and I am sure the former would have appreciated the modest aim of the latter as expressed in a certain letter to his publishers: "I would endeavour to bring in some of the glamour – the magic of sunshine, and green things, and calm waters – if I could." Was not Constable saying much the same thing when he declared that the qualities he aimed at in his pictures were "light, dews, breezes, bloom and freshness"? And was it not he who proclaimed the ideal of "the calm sunshine of the heart"? These things, indeed, were his strength and resistance against the painful lack of recognition which he so long endured, for he was never popular in his lifetime nor commercially successful. Of his specifically Essex paintings the following are among the best-known: *Dedham Vale* (Victoria and Albert Museum), *Hadleigh Castle, The Corn-*

field (National Gallery), *Harwich, Sea and Lighthouse* (Tate Gallery), and *The Cottage in the Cornfield* (Victoria and Albert). Constable died in 1837; and just over a hundred years later his famous Flatford Mill, together with Willy Lot's Cottage, were acquired by the Council for the Promotion of Field Studies as one of their first Centres – a choice which surely would have delighted the great painter.

Sir George Clausen lived for some of the best and most productive years of his long life in Essex, in the little village of Widdington, off the main Cambridge to Stortford road, and in Duton Hill, between Thaxted and Dunmow. Clausen succeeded to an altogether exceptional degree in getting on to his canvases those subtle atmospheric effects in which Essex excels, but he was also a notable recorder of the Essex rural folk and their way of life. *The Girl at the Gate* (1890), a poignant picture now in the Tate Gallery, is a case in point. Picturesque poverty, the cynic might call the theme of such paintings; but I for one would prefer to call it Clausen's sensitive appreciation of that elusive mixture of joy and sorrow which characterised the Essex cottager's life towards the end of the nineteenth century and the beginning of the twentieth. Like Constable he was an example of the complete countryman. As one critic said of him, he literally followed the plough, sketching the worker in action and afterwards utilising the sketches in his studio. There was in him a certain kinship with Millet, whom he greatly admired, but he lacked that painter's piety, which anyhow would have been quite out of place in any portrayal of the Essex labourer. What appeals most in Clausen, perhaps, is his constant care to reveal the humanity of the Essex labourer: it shows in all his pictures of the rural working life – in *Gossip on the Road,* for instance, where the horseman is shown riding one of his horses as he takes them home down the lane after a day's work and talking back as he goes to the mower with his scythe over his shoulder: a summer scene, in fact, which tenderly but factually evokes the Essex labouring life.

All the same, there were times when Clausen chafed under the limitations of country life, as most artists do at some time or another, who need to sharpen their wits and feed their senses with a culture all too lacking in the life devoted to the care of stock and crop. I remember an old friend of Clausen's once telling me how he would sometimes walk down the hill from

Widdington to where the main Cambridge-London railway line runs under a bridge. There he would stand, leaning over the parapet, watching the trains come rattling past. When they had disappeared round the corner, under their plumes of smoke, so purposeful in their errand, so energetic, he would mutter: "Well, thank goodness there's *somebody* doesn't have to spend all his time in this benighted hole!" Then he would tramp contentedly up the hill to home again. Like Constable, too, he had a rare ability in the painting of skies and was fond of quoting Corot's saying that, as a young man painting from nature, he used to wish the clouds would stay still, so that he might draw their forms, until one day he realised how good it was that they did not stay still, for the thing to express in clouds was their sense of movement. Inevitably this later Academician had illuminating things to say about Constable. In his *Six Lectures on Painting,* for instance, I find the following: "The work of Constable touches on smaller things (than Turner's) and the more homely aspects of nature. He sees things at close quarters: his range is not so great. He felt the beauty of everyday nature, of trees and fields under the sky, and painted them with a clearness and a freedom from convention which were then new in art." And, since almost any Essex man must surely appreciate especially Constable's most characteristic *Elm Tree,* where one almost has the feeling that the rough bark would graze one's knuckles, I will quote Clausen's remarks in this particular connection. "I think (he says) one of the most difficult things in painting is to paint a tree. ... It is not so very difficult to copy a tree, but to paint it so as to make it live, to give us the impression of life that the tree gives us when we look at it in passing, is a thing that few can do well."

There have been, of course, many other artists associated with Essex; but these two, Constable and Clausen, were supreme; and if I mention two others, both from the last century, it is more out of a personal preference than for any intention to claim them as masters. One of these was Samuel Williams, who was born at Colchester in 1788 and apprenticed to a printer there. He also worked as an engraver in London, where he made his admirable drawings and blocks for Crosby's *Natural History, Hone's Everyday Book,* and others. But one of my own favourite examples of his work is the set of engravings he did for Jeffery Taylor's *The Farm: A New Account of Rural*

Tools and Produce. All the drawings here are not only excellent in themselves but very revealing of contemporary rural life and manners – especially "The Rent Audit" and "Saturday Night." These are certainly Essex drawings, and, for their period, they are surprisingly realistic in subject and conceived with a pleasant humour. Williams died in 1853. The remaining Essex artist to whom I shall refer was George Washington Brownlow. I confess I had not heard of this artist until the *Essex Review* published (Oct. 1947) a letter appealing for information concerning him, together with a couple of reproductions of charming studies of country children. It appears that although Brownlow died at Sudbury in 1876, at the age of forty-one, he was buried at Belchamp Walter, in Essex, "amid the sorrowing regret of nearly all the parishioners and a large company of friends from the district round." The note went on to say that an oil painting of his called *Moorhen's Nest* was in Sudbury Town Hall and that one Ted Baker, the miller's boy, served as model for the egg-stealing lad in the picture. At the first opportunity I went to Sudbury to see the painting for myself. I found it, hung regrettably high, over the doorway into the main hall. Nobody seemed to know anything about it, much less about the artist, though the attendant proudly informed me that "only the other week" somebody had come all the way from Australia to look at it because they had known Ted, the miller's boy. Brownlow evidently favoured scenes with a story, but at least in this case the story is beautifully subjected to the painting itself. All in all, it seems a pity that so far nobody has come forward with any information in response to the letter in the *Essex Review.* Brownlow and Williams were both Essex artists of whom one would like to know a great deal more.

Writers in Essex have been many and various, ranging from Purchas to William Morris and from Suckling to Tennyson; and the most I can do here is to refer to those whose associations with the county have been in some way outstanding. Of Samuel Purchas, who was born at Thaxted in 1577, and of Sir John Suckling, who was born at Witham in 1613, there is little to say in any case, because little is known. Both are more revered today than read: some of Sir John's sprightly, witty verses ornament the more representative anthologies, and extracts from *Purchas His Pilgrims* occasionally appear in students' examination papers. The one interesting fact we know about Purchas is that at one time he was vicar of Eastwood, a village near Leigh, and so it is possible that it was his contact with the Leigh sailors and his lively interest in their tales of exploration and adventure that induced him to write his famous book or so it might seem from the tale, included therein, of Andrew Battell, of Leigh, who was the first European to bring home authentic news of the interior of Africa. But in the end perhaps the most interesting thing to record about both these writers is that the family name is still a common one in the districts of their birth.

Of Francis Quarles I would like to write rather more fully: not that he is so much more widely read today or that we know for certain so much more about his life, but that there is a peculiar charm about the Essex associations of this poet of the lugubrious titles. Quarles was not only born in Essex, near Romford, in 1592, but he wrote some of his best work here, which would seem to argue an admirable preference on his part. His *Emblems,* on which his greatest fame rests, was written whilst staying at the home of another, if lesser, Essex poet, Edward Benlowes, of Finchingfield. The two may have been attracted to one another by a common trait of recklessness, for did not Quarles, when he was a student of law at Lincoln's Inn, sell his Inn-of-Court gown to buy himself a lute, and did not Benlowes squander his money to such an extent that, when he died in Oxford, compassionate scholar friends had to find money to bury him? Anyhow, at some time Quarles was a guest at Brent Hall, Benlowes' Finchingfield home, and tradition insists that he was in the habit of meandering in a nearby copse seeking the inspiration which flowered in the *Emblems.* Certainly there is a preface to another of his books which confirms the fact that he was in the habit of so seeking his inspiration. This particular preface, or "Address to the Reader," is in his *Shepheard's Oracles*; and, although it is signed by the printer, really it is supposed to have been written by Izaak Walton. There are qualities in these two men that chime together, and it might well be that the beloved angler contributed this preface to his friend's book. Here is how it begins: "He in a summer's morning about that hour when the great Eye of Heaven first opens itself to give light to us mortals, walking a gentle pace towards a Brook whose springhead was not far distant from his peaceful habitation, fitted with angles, lines and flyes, flyes proper for that season, it being the fruitful month of May, intending with all diligence to beguile the timorous trout with which that watery element abounded, observed a more than common concourse of shepherds all bending their unwearied steps towards a pleasant Meadow where was a large arbour whose walls were made of the yielding willow and smooth beech boughs, covered over with sycamore leaves and honeysuckles." It is pleasant, and no harm done, to fancy that in similar mood and a not dissimilar place Quarles found the inspiration for his *Emblems*. Brent Hall stands a little outside the village, mellow and comely beyond the ordinary, and not far away is a copse called Long Almond Grove, where there are "honeysuckles" and the nightingale sings. I for one shall go on supposing that it was here the poet came, "walking a gentle pace."

Other poets who called Essex home include Mathew Prior, who was born at Hatfield Broadoak, author of one immortal song ("The merchant, to secure his treasure") and some of the finest epigrams in the language; Tennyson, who resided at High Beech; Thomas Hood, who wrote his revolutionary "Song of the Shirt" at Luke House, on the Wanstead Flats; William Morris, who spent most of his youth at Woodford and never ceased to sing the praises of the nearby Forest (especially its unique hornbeans); and John Clare, known popularly as the Ploughman Poet, who, though a Northamptonshire man, spent some of the most distressful years of his life at Fair Mead House, which was then a private asylum in the Forest and which he left "in a hurry" on July 20, 1841, tramping four days to his home in Northamptonshire. Clare had been made much of by fashionable society, more for his being a ploughman who wrote poetry than for his being a poet who happened once to have driven the plough; but later, when he was often deranged in mind and always lonely, he had little comfort from that quarter; and his long march from the asylum, with nothing to eat but wayside grass "which seemed to taste something like bread" and nowhere to sleep but the ground, must surely rank among the most pathetic journeys ever man made out of Fssex. On his arrival home he wrote to Dr Allen, the founder of the asylum, to explain his hurried departure. "... I can be miserably happy in any situation and any place," he said, "and could have stayed in yours on the Forest if any of my friends had noticed me or come to see me. But the greatest annoyance in such places as yours are those servants styled keepers, who often assumed as much authority over me as if I had been their prisoner; and not liking to quarrel I put up with it till I was weary of the place altogether. So I heard the voice of freedom, and could have travelled to York with a penny loaf and a pint of beer; for I should not have been fagged in body, only one of my old shoes had nearly lost the sole before I started, and let in the water and silt the first day, and made me crippled and lame to the end of my journey." Almost every one of Clare's innumerable poems has in it something rare and fresh and individual – a quality of greatness, in fact, which has only recently come to be recognised at all widely; but it was while he was in the Forest asylum that he wrote his finest and most terrible poem, "I am; yet what I am none cares or knows," a poem disciplined out of the very depths of human suffering.

It is not generally known that William Byrd, of whom Dr Edmund Fellowes wrote, "It may even be right to place him at the head of the sixteenth-century composers of all countries," lived for many years in Essex. Certainly he was already fifty years old when he finally abandoned his position as organist of the Chapel Royal and came to settle on the property he had acquired at Stondon Massey, but he had still thirty years to live and it was during these years of rural retirement that he wrote much of the music which earned for him the title of "Father of Musick." Nothing now remains of Stondon Place, where he lived; and, indeed, the only actual memorial to this great man who thus honoured the county is a memorial tablet which was placed on the south wall of the church there on the occasion of his tercentenary. It is not even certain that Byrd (who died in 1623) was buried in Stondon Church; for although he expressed a wish that this might be so, the Parish Registers of 1623 no longer exist. His years of retirement in Essex were not without their disturbances. Byrd seems to have had an unfortunate capacity for acquiring properties, either by grant or purchase, with doubtful titles, in consequence of which he was often involved in litigation. Then, too, he was an adherent to the older traditions of the church as opposed to the Reformation (though he held positions in the service of the Reformed Anglican Church) and on at least one occasion a bill was issued against him for being a recusant. Nevertheless, he was undoubtedly honoured. We know that Morley, the great madrigalist, spoke of him as a man "never without reverence to be named among musicians"; and so, with Dr Fellowes, "we may hope that the closing years of Byrd's long life were passed in comparative peace, even though there are hints of trouble of some kind within his own family circle."

These closing years were certainly spent at Stondon, and Dr Fellowes thinks it most probable that his three great masses, as well as other of his noble music, may have been composed at Stondon Place. ... And here I trust I may be forgiven if I relate a personal experience. It happened that at the time of Byrd's tercentenary I was living in an Essex village well to the north of Stondon Massey. His music had not yet won general recognition again, after its long period of oblivion; and certainly I was no more familiar with it than most. One night I dreamed I was in a cathedral where a choir and orchestra were giving a public performance of some work which was new to me. All was clear and precise and intelligible, as if I had actually been present; and I remember that when I woke up whole phrases of the music remained with me and I could have written down some of the words. During the performance I had turned to my neighbour and asked in a whisper what the music was. "Byrd's Mass," he replied. Next morning, when I opened the newspaper, I found there an account of the first performance in Norwich Cathedral of one of Byrd's recently discovered masses. No doubt it was all pure coincidence and capable of an entirely rational explanation; yet how one would like to believe otherwise!

Gustav Holst, I think, would almost certainly have agreed there was more to this odd incident than the rationalist might suppose, for he was an unsentimental advocate of the power of the occult. For some years this distinguished composer was a well-known figure in Essex: he lived for a while at Thaxted and again at Brook End in Easton Park. Perhaps it would be stretching a point, however, to claim Holst as an Essex musician, for although to my knowledge at least one of his major works (the opera *The Perfect Fool*) was written in the house overlooking the old Guild Hall in Thaxted, he never liked to be away for long from his sound-proof room in London. Nevertheless, he often organised the music for the Thaxted church festivals and once he brought his pupils down from Morley College to sing there. Thaxted, in fact, where one of the last of the

traditional Essex folk-singers was to be heard and where the
Morris dancers danced in the streets, would seem to have been
the ideal rural retreat for a composer who did so much to found
a nationalist school of music in this country.

b. Various

One of the oddest of Essex worthies was surely Sir John
Hawkwood, who was born at Sible Hedingham round about the
year 1320 and won a curious fame as a soldier of fortune in
Italy, where he died in 1394. The Hawkwood family must have
been one of some distinction in the locality, if the hawks which
decorate the tower and other portions of Sible Hedingham
church are, as is supposed, an indication that they contributed
largely to the cost of its construction. There is also a well-
endowed Hawkwood charity, both here and at Castle Hedingham. And yet the legend persists that John was the second son
of a local tanner; but perhaps this is not so contradictory as it
may seem, since William the Conqueror was also the grandson
of a tanner. In any case, John entered the army, served with a
company of archers in France, and at Poitiers so distinguished
himself that he was promoted to a captaincy. When, ultimately,
the English forces in France were disbanded and, after the
manner of the time, left to fend for themselves as best they
might, John, instead of returning to Essex, recruited a company
of archers from the demobilised soldiers and proceeded to hire
himself out to anybody who might need (and was willing to pay
for) his and his men's services. There followed a series of skir-
mishes and battles which finally landed Hawkwood and his
army in Italy. The story of these wandering mercenaries, whose
shining breast-plates (for Hawkwood was a stern disciplinarian)
earned them the name among the Italians of the White
Company, reads like wilder fancies of a romantic novelist. The
Duke of Milan, for instance, was so much his admirer that he
gave him his daughter Domnia in marriage; whilst Pope Greg-
ory XI, in whose service Hawkwood performed some of his most
amazing exploits, addressed him in terms of affection and
rewarded him with a considerable property in the Romagna. At
his death, Sir John (it is not known exactly how or from whom
he received his knighthood) was honoured with a magnificent
monument in Florence Cathedral. Of another monument to his
memory in Sible Hedingham church, Fuller says, "his Cœno-

taph, or honorary tombe, which sometime stood in the Parish
Church (arched over, and, in allusion to his name, berebussed
with *Hawkes* flying in a *Wood*) is now quite flown away and
abolished." Not quite, however; for the recess that contained it
still remains in the south wall, surmounted by a crocketed
canopy and decorated with the familiar hawk.

More gentle by far and, as I understand the word, by far
more worthy was John Ray, whose only pillaging was among the
plant and insect life of the fields and who established his world-
wide fame as a naturalist by, for the most part, biding quietly at
home in Black Notley. "Of late years," he wrote in 1702, when
he was near his end, "I have diverted myself by searching out
the various species of insects to he found hereabout, but I have
confined myself chiefly to two or three sorts, viz. Papilios,
diurnal and nocturnal, Beetles, Bees and Spiders. Of the first of
these I have found about 300 kinds, and there are still remaining many more undiscovered by me, and all within the compass
of a few miles. How many, then, may we reasonably conjecture
are to be found in the whole world? The Beetles are a tribe near
as numerous as these, and the Flies of all sorts are not fewer. I
have now given over my inquisition by reason of my disability
and my approaching end, which I pray God fit me for." But Ray
had already established his reputation as a botanist by his
system of classification of plants, a system which, when subse-
quently revised by himself, formed the basis of all plant classification for years to come. In preparation for this task he had
made botanical journeys covering nearly the whole of Britain,
either alone or in the company of an amateur zoologist named
Francis Willoughby, whose early death deprived Ray of his
closest friend and enriched him with an annuity of £170,
whereby he was enabled to spend the last twenty-five years of
his life in his home at Black Notley, engaged in the continuous
pursuit of his studies.

Botanists, like gardeners, are often of a mild and philosophic
disposition; and Ray was no exception. The increasing illness
which finally compelled him (if desire had not persuaded him) to
remain at home was an ulceration of the legs. It is indicative of
the state of medicine at the time that this learned man should
have come to the conclusion that his complaint was caused by
"invisible insects making their burrows under and nestling in
the cutis, spreading in spots around which may be their nests,

like anthills, they seeming to be gregarious." But if Ray could no longer go out to the world, the world certainly came to him: fellow scientists from far afield corresponded with him and it was often a curious cargo with which the Black Notley carrier drove up to the door of Dewlands on his bumpy return from Braintree. There are in Black Notley today two reminders of this pious and indefatigible naturalist: the blacksmith's forge (its hatch still opening on to the quiet country lane) where his father carried on his humble trade, and a grandiose monument in the churchyard. When the chancel end of the church was destroyed by bombs in 1943, Ray's tomb was also badly damaged; but both have since been restored, the latter by the generosity of members of the Ray Society. The roving visitor may therefore once again read (though in Latin) how:

Here in this narrow tomb, this marble span,
Lies all that death could snatch from this great man;
His body moulders in its native clay,
While o'er wide worlds his works their beams display,
As bright and everlasting as the day.

Or he may prefer, as I do, the measured words of Ray's early biographer, Derham. "In his dealings no man more strictly just; in his conversation no man more humble, courteous, and affable; towards God, no man more devout; and towards the poor and distressed, no man more compassionate and charitable, according to his abilities." From which it may be gathered that our Black Notley scientist was also something of a saint.

There was nothing of the saint, however, about Dick Turpin. The strict realist would probably proclaim him sinner out and out. But popular opinion, and Essex popular opinion in particular, has decreed otherwise. Never was lawlessness so flagrantly canonised. The number of stories, ballads, verses, legends, anecdotes and so forth that have accumulated about the name of this Essex highwayman is surely without equal. His famous ride to York even developed into a national fable. Yet what, as far as we know them, are the plain facts? Turpin was born, in 1706 or thereabouts, at Hempstead, a village not far from Saffron Walden. The actual house he was born in is a matter for some speculation; but the local bid is for the village inn, of which his father was sometime keeper. He was apprenticed to a butcher and almost at once gave an indication of the kind of life he intended to follow by cattle stealing. After this early escapade he fled and was next heard of in the role of smuggler in the Rochford and Dengie Hundreds. At the height of his career he centred his predatory activities on the Forest, which provided him and his scoundrelly gang with a very convenient hiding-place. Nobody was safe with his life, let alone his goods, on the highways adjacent to the Forest. Murder may never have been part of his avowed technique, but he seems to have been guilty of it all the same, though it was for horse-stealing that he was finally brought to trial and hanged in 1739. The worst of his success was that it bred a similar courage (for this he certainly had) in others, so that for some time after his death it remained hazardous for people to travel unless in company or with an armed guard. (One footpad, it is reported, was actually shot, in 1765, by an armed guard employed to accompany hay wagons returning through the Essex lanes from London.) Whence, then, this persistent legend that has consistently attached itself to the name of Dick Turpin? To some extent, I suppose, Harrison Ainsworth may have been responsible, though I am more inclined to think he merely gave a vivid and dramatic expression to an already existing popular sentiment. To some extent, also, Turpin's dexterity as a horseman is responsible: his name is inseparable in the public mind from that of his horse, Black Bess, who seems to have been as skilful in leaping a moat as her master was in picking a pocket. But perhaps, after all, it was Turpin's undeniable courage that endeared him so. As Dr Johnson said: "We have more respect for a man who robs boldly on the highway, than for a fellow who jumps out of a ditch and knocks you down behind your back. Courage is a quality so necessary for maintaining virtue, that it is always respected, even when it is associated with vice."

The names of Sir Harvey and John Elwes, uncle and nephew respectively, are not much remembered even in their native Essex. Successively they owned several estates, including one at Ashen (Claret Hall), and were known as the Misers of Ashen. Miserliness of an incredible order provided the sole zest and purpose of their lives, although, to do him justice, the nephew seems to have caught the complaint from his uncle. I know of only one substantial account of the strange habits of these two eighteenth-century misers, and so I make no excuse for copying

direct from Wright's well-known history of the county. "Sir
Harvey at all times wore a black velvet cap, a worn-out full-
dress suit of clothes, and an old great-coat, with worsted stockings drawn up over his knees. He rode a thin thoroughbred
horse and her rider seemed as if a gust of wind would have
blown them away together. He would walk backwards and
forwards in the old hall, during unfavourable weather, to save
the expense of a fire; and, if a neighbour called on business,
would strike a light with a tinder-box, and, putting a single
stick on the grate, would not add another till the first was
nearly consumed. ... He was timid, shy, and diffident in the
extreme: of a thin, spare habit of body, and without a friend
upon the earth. The hoarding up and counting his money formed
his greatest joy. Next to that was partridge setting, at which he
was so great an adept that he has been known to take five
hundred brace of birds in one season. He and his whole household, consisting of one man and two maids, lived entirely upon
partridges." Not unnaturally, he was robbed in the end, for he
always kept several thousand pounds in the house; but the
thieves – the Thaxted gang, as they were called – were eventually caught. Sir Harvey, however, would not appear against
them. "I have lost my money," he said, "and will not lose my
time also." At his death, the estates were inherited by his
nephew, John, who carried his uncle's parsimony even further.
Eventually he settled in a farmhouse, on the borders of the
Forest. To tell of him would be but to repeat another version of
his uncle's story. Let Wright's final words about him therefore
be our last view of this unworthy worthy of Essex. "For six
weeks previous to his death, on the 18th of November, 1789, he
would go to rest in his clothes; and he was found one morning
fast asleep, in bed, with his shoes on his feet, his stick in his
hand, and an old torn hat upon his head."

My last Essex worthy is an eighteenth-century knight who
has always intrigued me – and eluded me – ever since I first
came to live in his parish. Muilman described Sir John
Marshall, of Sculpins, in Finchingfield, as the man "who
performed the last piece of the old British hospitality in the
parish. He kept open house every Thursday in the year, and
provided a spacious bowling green for the weekly entertainment
of his neighbours." When I first knew Sculpins it was a diminished timber-framed farmhouse up a cart-track on the outskirts

of the parish. In the lonely green ride that led away from the magpie house one could always be sure of finding the first drifts of white violets, the first paigles and periwinkles, and the first golden willow catkins caught in a mesh of buzzing bees. Whatever had been Sculpins' fame in the past, it was just a small farmhouse now, but it somehow kept an atmosphere of appeal. In the village, too, there were persistent stories of this prodigal menage, which seemed to have had the very habit of display and hospitality fastened on to it by the illustrious Sir John. According to the late Miss Eliza Vaughan, whose tireless research into the history of this parish offers an example of how such things should be done, "there was maintained such lavish hospitality that local tales are still repeated in the village" (she was writing at the beginning of this century) "of his famous bowling parties, whereunto all the gay and fashionable world resorted every week, and his ponderous coach, drawn by four powerful grey horses, that used to crash down the now green bridle-path to the church on bygone Sabbaths." It is this magnificent Sunday equipage, even more than the bowling green and feasts, that has stuck in the village mind – as if for the villagers this was real, and so remembered, whilst the rest was only rumour (to them), and so forgotten. Yet I am puzzled by this Sculpins legend. There does not seem enough substance in it to warrant the warmth with which it is remembered. Something has been lost, and, try as I may, I cannot find it. And indeed, I doubt if now it ever will be found. Sculpins itself was all but swallowed by a great airfield which was built in the vicinity for the last war, and the village has found other things to talk about than this elusive example of one of the last of the great liberal gentlemen of Essex.

CHAPTER V

Concluding View

THE signpost at the entrance to the chase points a single white finger across the fields and says: "Public Green Lane leading to Little London." But the signpost lies. Its invitation was acceptable enough in those days (already another age, they seem) before Lord Reith, acting under the threat of invasion in a second world war, ordered all directional signs and place-names to be removed (to the confusion, as it turned out, rather of the defenders than of any invaders), but nobody, from choice, would follow its inviting finger today. Of course, we were pleased to see the signpost back again: it was like an old friend returning after long absence. For we in Essex are proud of our footpath signs. Long ago our county council had won golden opinions for the thoroughness with which it signposted and so safeguarded those field tracks and right-of-ways which date back to the days when farmhands had to walk to their work and naturally chose the quickest and shortest way to do it – bequests to us, as one might say, from the villagers of long ago. And now, to see the signposts returning seemed a happy augury: we should get our rights back again after all. And so the little white finger went up: "Public Green Lane leading to Little London." But is a lane public when its gates are kept padlocked and festooned with barbed wire? Part of the way consisted of an ancient "dool," which is the old Essex name for a path across a ploughed field which may not by law be erased. But is it a dool any longer when its edges have been ploughed to the width of a few inches, requiring the skill of a tight-rope walker to negotiate it? As for the greenness, this has quite departed. Instead of daisied turf, walled in with wild roses and canopied with the song of skylarks, the roaming pigs have left a slough of mud resembling the bottom of a clay pond from which the water has been drained. From springy green turf to slimy ooze and from skylark song to pig-grunt – but I will refrain from drawing an obvious, though possibly too facile, moral: it is enough to say that the public green lane leading to Little London is no longer either public or green, or even a lane at all.

And the tale of this deceiving signpost could be repeated all over Essex. Nor is it only our footpaths and green rides that have been stolen away from us. What about some of our Commons? I think of Morris Green, for instance, where no doubt the village dancers once trod to the tune of pipe and strings, and where, when these fashions passed, the cottagers were at least free to keep their geese and goats; it is all ploughed up now, and contributes, however meagrely, to our national larder. But a recitation of such instances would be tedious and no doubt these things had to be. At any rate, we tolerated them in such a belief and foolishly put our trust in the promise that our commons, like our footpaths, would be restored to us in good time. It was decreed, for example, that farmers when they ploughed up a right-of-way across one of their fields should provide the walker with an alternative route: thus the public ownership of these ancient inheritances would be secured. But farmers were priority men, and still are; and so they were not always called to account when, out of laziness or sheer lack of concern for the interest and welfare of others, they disregarded such an order. So the footpaths have disappeared, and is it surprising if we begin to doubt whether they will ever come back again? The things we thought we were tolerating out of a temporary necessity have turned out to be no temporary renouncement at all but a downright theft of the rights of the common man.

Indeed, the trend of recent events more than confirms us in our pessimism. Take a look round the countryside at some of the things that are happening in Essex today. I have already said that, quite apart from the Forest, the county is surprisingly well supplied with trees; but I should have used the past tense. The trees are disappearing at an alarming rate; and, what is worse, none are being planted in their place. Many a good woodland and productive field had to be grubbed up to make way for one or other of the airfields which scarred the county during the war. Some at least of these fields have been put back into production; but how shall the oak and ash, good trees in their prime of a hundred and fifty years, be put back? And now, as if this were not evil enough, since trees, quite apart from their beauty, are an essential concommitant of good husbandry as conservers of water in a dry land and homes for insect-devouring birds, the remaining trees are going down by the thousand. I watch the great timber-wagons go lumbering past my house every day, each bearing its noble, stricken corpse to the nearest railway station or timber-yard; and the procession of chopped and mighty hulks is repeated everywhere. If this goes on much longer, the fair Essex arable will soon be as bare as the back of one's hand. How far away seems that day when the hedgers and ditchers, going their winter round of the fields, saved, out of foresight and something near affection for the bounty which nature afforded, any good saplings they happened to come upon – not for their own use or even for their master's, but for the generations still unborn? But the hedger of today spares nothing: his orders, by the look of things, are to hack the lot to the ground. But what does it matter, anyway? Presently there will be no hedges with saplings in them to spare; for the trend is now all in favour of laying land to land again, as was done when the old open-field system gave way to enclosure and agriculture took its first slow step towards becoming just another industry. Indeed, as a recognised industry already, I suppose it is unreasonable to expect anything but a short-time policy in agriculture today. If it provides the farmer with a ready solution to his difficulties (scarce labour and dear) to grub out his hedges and plough in his ditches, it would be foolish to expect him not to avail himself of it. As an industrialist, like any other, what has he to do, for instance, with such elusive factors as field-names? Bell Rope Piece – why should he care that such a name harks back to the days when the rent of this particular field was set aside for the upkeep of the ropes in the church belfry? Or Vineyards – what should he mind that this remembers the time when Essex grew its own grapes and made its own wine? Or that Tuffs is the field from which, centuries ago, the villagers were permitted to cut their turves for firing? Moot Pightle, Slipe, Shallow Shot, Dow Pits, Moot Field, to take a handful of field-names from one village only, are instances of the endearing fact that the local history of this island is as likely to be found written in furrow and sod as in the ink of our learned historians. But why should the industrialised and harrassed farmer be expected to bother about this? Hasten the day (his attitude seems to suggest) when such names will be replaced by the neat and convenient formulæ, of A/43, B/62, and C/441.

I instance these developments in the Essex countryside because they seem to me indicative of more than themselves. It used to be axiomatic with the good farmer that he farmed as much for tomorrow as for today, as much for his son and his son's son as for himself; and the knowledge was never far absent from all his actions that he must hand on the land at his death in at least as good a heart as when he inherited it. That kind of husbandry is no more. And so these developments in the Essex countryside are indicative of a moral as well as a physical change. I look at the weather-beaten features of some of the old men whose pictures appear in this book, men of the Essex of yesterday, and I am compelled to ask myself whence comes the excellence which they reveal – that quality of, shall we say, tender strength? These were men who grew up with none of the advantages which today are taken for granted. They were not educated, their working hours were long and hard, their wages were small, they knew nothing of those social and domestic amenities which we find so essential, and their horizon, both physically and mentally, was limited by the furthest field they could see from their own back door. And yet – but look at their faces and these will tell better than I can what quality it was they possessed in such liberal measure that we less and less possess today. They were men of endurance. Above all, they were *individuals*. "Always get over a stile," said Richard Jefferies, and it is a saying capable of more interpretations than one. These were men who never could resist a stile, and by climbing over it they discovered a whole host of things that are not to be discovered on the highway. They it was whose hobnailed feet trod out the paths across the fields to which the white fingerpost now invites in vain; it might as well not be there. We have all got to keep to the highway these days. Even in Essex.

Index